General editor: Graham Handley MA Ph.D.

Brodie's Notes on William Shakespeare's

Othello

Peter Washington MA B.Litt.
Senior Tutor and Deputy Head, The Graduate Centre, Middlesex Polytechnic

Pan Books London, Sydney and Auckland

First published 1985 by Pan Books Ltd
This revised edition published 1990 by Pan Books Ltd,
Cavaye Place, London SW10 9PG
9 8 7 6 5 4 3 2 1
© Pan Books Ltd 1990
ISBN 0 330 50284 0
Photoset by Parker Typesetting Service, Leicester
Printed and bound in Great Britain by
Richard Clay Ltd, Bungay, Suffolk

Contents

Line references in these Notes are to the
Arden Shakespeare: Othello,
but as references are given to particular
acts and scenes, the Notes may be used
with any edition of the play.

Preface

This student revision aid is based on the principle that in any close examination of Shakespeare's plays 'the text's the thing'. Seeing a performance, or listening to a tape or record of a performance, is essential and is in itself a valuable and stimulating experience in understanding and appreciation. However, a real evaluation of Shakespeare's greatness, of his universality and of the nature of his literary and dramatic art, can only be achieved by constant application to the texts of the plays themselves. These revised editions of Brodie's Notes are intended to supplement that process through detailed critical commentary.

The first aim of each book is to fix the whole play in the reader's mind by providing a concise summary of the plot, relating it back, where appropriate, to its source or sources. Subsequently the book provides a summary of each scene, followed by *critical comments*. These may convey its importance in the dramatic structure of the play, creation of atmosphere, indication of character development, significance of figurative language etc, and they will also explain or paraphrase difficult words or phrases and identify meaningful references. At the end of each act revision questions are set to test the student's specific and broad understanding and appreciation of the play.

An extended critical commentary follows this scene by scene analysis. This embraces such major elements as characterization, imagery, the use of blank verse and prose, soliloquies and other aspects of the play which the editor considers need close attention. The paramount aim is to send the reader back to the text. The book concludes with a series of revision questions which require a detailed knowledge of the play; the first of these has notes by the editor of what *might* be included in a written answer. The intention is to stimulate and to guide; the whole emphasis of this commentary is to encourage the student's *involvement* in the play, to develop disciplined critical responses and thus promote personal enrichment through the imaginative experience of our greatest writer.

Graham Handley

Shakespeare and the Elizabethan playhouse

William Shakespeare was born in Stratford-upon-Avon in 1564, and there are reasons to suppose that he came from a relatively prosperous family. He was probably educated at Stratford Grammar School and, at the age of eighteen, married Anne Hathaway, who was twenty-six. They had three children, a girl born shortly after their marriage, followed by twins in 1585 (the boy died in 1596). It seems likely that Shakespeare left for London shortly after a company of visiting players had visited Stratford in 1585, for by 1592 – according to the jealous testimony of one of his fellow-writers Robert Greene – he was certainly making his way both as actor and dramatist. The theatres were closed because of the plague in 1593; when they reopened Shakespeare worked with the Lord Chamberlain's Men, later the King's Men, and became a shareholder in each of the two theatres with which he was most closely associated, the Globe and the Blackfriars. He later purchased New Place, a considerable property in his home town of Stratford, to which he retired in 1611; there he entertained his great contemporary Ben Jonson (1572–1637) and the poet Michael Drayton (1563–1631). An astute businessman, Shakespeare lived comfortably in the town until his death in 1616.

This is a very brief outline of the life of our greatest writer, for little more can be said of him with certainty, though the plays – and poems – are living witness to the wisdom, humanity and many-faceted nature of the man. He was both popular and successful as a dramatist, perhaps less so as an actor. He probably began work as a dramatist in the late 1580s, by collaborating with other playwrights and adapting old plays, and by 1598 Francis Meres was paying tribute to his excellence in both comedy and tragedy. His first original play was probably *Love's Labour's Lost* (1590) and while the theatres were closed during the plague he wrote his narrative poems *Venus and Adonis* (1593) and *The Rape of Lucrece* (1594). The sonnets were almost certainly written in the 1590s, though not published until 1609; the first 126 seem to be addressed to a young man who was his friend and patron, while the rest are concerned with the 'dark lady'.

The dating of Shakespeare's plays has exercised scholars ever since the publication of the First Folio (1623), which listed them as comedies, histories and tragedies. It seems more important to look at them chronologically as far as possible, in order to trace Shakespeare's considerable development as a dramatist. The first period, say to the middle of the 1590s, included such plays as *Love's Labour's Lost*, *The Comedy of Errors*, *Richard III*, *The Taming of the Shrew*, *Romeo and Juliet* and *Richard II*. These early plays embrace the categories listed in the First Folio, so that Shakespeare the craftsman is evident in his capacity for variety of subject and treatment. The next phase includes *A Midsummer's Night's Dream*, *The Merchant of Venice*, *Henry IV Parts 1 and 2*, *Henry V* and *Much Ado About Nothing*, as well as *Julius Caesar*, *As You Like It* and *Twelfth Night*. These are followed, in the early years of the 17th century, by his great tragic period: *Hamlet*, *Othello*, *King Lear* and *Macbeth*, with *Antony and Cleopatra* and *Coriolanus* belonging to 1607–09. The final phase embraces the romances (1610–13), *Cymbeline*, *The Tempest* and *The Winter's Tale* and the historical play *Henry VIII*.

Each of these revision aids will place the individual text under examination in the chronology of the remarkable dramatic output that spanned twenty years from the early 1590s to about 1613. The practical theatre for which Shakespeare wrote and acted derived from the inn courtyards in which performances had taken place, the few playhouses in his day being modelled on their structure. They were circular or hexagonal in shape, allowing the balconies and boxes around the walls full view of the stage. This large stage, which had no scenery, jutted out into the pit, the most extensive part of the theatre, where the poorer people – the 'groundlings' – stood. There was no roof (though the Blackfriars, used from 1608 onwards, was an indoor theatre) and thus bad weather meant no performance. Certain plays were acted at court, and these private performances normally marked some special occasion. Costumes, often rich ones, were used, and music was a common feature, with musicians on or under the stage; this sometimes had additional features, for example a trapdoor to facilitate the entry of a ghost. Women were barred by law from appearing on stage, and all female parts were played by boy actors; this undoubtedly explains the many instances in Shakespeare where a woman has to conceal her identity by disguising

herself as a man, e.g. Rosalind in *As You Like It*, Viola in *Twelfth Night*.

Shakespeare and his contemporaries often adapted their plays from sources in history and literature, extending an incident or a myth or creating a dramatic narrative from known facts. They were always aware of their own audiences, and frequently included topical references, sometimes of a satirical flavour, which would appeal to – and be understood by – the ground-lings as well as their wealthier patrons who occupied the boxes. Shakespeare obviously learned much from his fellow dramatists and actors, being on good terms with many of them. Ben Jonson paid generous tribute to him in the lines prefaced to the First Folio of Shakespeare's plays:

Thou art a monument without a tomb,
And art alive still, while thy book doth live
And we have wits to read, and praise to give.

Among his contemporaries were Thomas Kyd (1558–94) and Christopher Marlowe (1564–93). Kyd wrote *The Spanish Tragedy*, the revenge motif here foreshadowing the much more sophis-ticated treatment evident in *Hamlet*, while Marlowe evolved the 'mighty line' of blank verse, a combination of natural speech and elevated poetry. The quality and variety of Shakespeare's blank verse owes something to the innovatory brilliance of Marlowe, but carries the stamp of individuality, richness of association, technical virtuosity and, above all, the genius of imaginative power.

The texts of Shakespeare's plays are still rich sources for scholars, and the editors of these revision aids have used the Arden editions of Shakespeare, which are regarded as pre-eminent for their scholarly approach. They are strongly recom-mended for advanced students, but other editions, like The New Penguin Shakespeare, The New Swan, The Signet are all good annotated editions currently available. A reading list of selected reliable works on the play being studied is provided at the end of each commentary and students are advised to turn to these as their interest in the play deepens.

Literary terms used in these notes

A few specialist usages are given below, but where there is a full explanation of a term in either the *textual notes* or *critical commentary* (e.g. the section on *oxymoron*) it is not defined here.

iambic pentameter This is the staple line of English narrative and dramatic poetry. 'Pentameter' indicates that there are five beats, feet or stresses in the line. Iambs are feet in which there is a short syllable followed by a long, or an unstressed followed by a stressed. 'Without' is an iamb, for example.

irony The conveyance of meaning by words whose literal sense is the opposite of that implied.

dramatic irony This occurs when a character is unaware of the true significance of his words or actions but other characters on stage, as well as the reader and the audience, know exactly what is happening.

metaphor This is a figure of speech in which two things are not merely compared (as in a simile) but identified. It is not introduced by 'like' or 'as'.

oxymoron See special section on this p.116

catharsis A word used by Aristotle to describe the effect of tragedy on the audience. According to the context it can mean either purging or purification.

hubris Another of Aristotle's terms from the *Poetics*, hubris is the kind of blind pride characteristic of the tragic hero.

The play

Plot

Othello is the Moorish general charged by the Venetians to defend Cyprus against the Turks. Cassio is his lieutenant. Othello has recently and secretly married Desdemona. Iago, who claims to have a number of reasons for hating Othello, including his frustration at not being appointed lieutenant, conspires against both Othello and Cassio with Roderigo, a foolish Venetian gentleman who is in love with Desdemona, and who has paid Iago to intercede with her. By making Othello suspect Desdemona and the handsome Cassio of committing adultery, Iago induces Othello to plot their deaths, using as evidence of the adultery a handkerchief given by Othello to Desdemona, and purloined by Emilia (Iago's wife) at his request. When, after Othello has killed Desdemona, Emilia discovers Iago's scheme she reveals it, causing her own death and Iago's capture. Stricken by this revelation and the horror of his deed, Othello kills himself.

This is one of Shakespeare's simplest and neatest plots and it can be reduced to a formula: Iago, seeking revenge, brings about the deaths of Othello and Desdemona, but encompasses his own downfall in the process. In certain respects, therefore, the play conforms to a type common in its period: the revenge drama, in which one character exacts through violence what he sees as justice, at the expense of others. The classic example of revenge tragedy is *Hamlet*, in which the hero avenges the murder of his father. In *Othello*, however, the revenge pattern is complicated by two things: first that the revenger is the play's villain (Iago), and second by the fact that he seems to have no very good motive for his actions, beyond spite. Iago's absence of motive is echoed in the hero himself, who seems uncertain at the end of the play whether the killing of Desdemona can be regarded as a just 'sacrifice' (his word) or a revengeful crime. So it is that in the first words of Act V Scene 2 he dwells upon the 'cause' of his action. It can be said that Iago is both successful in his plot, in that he brings about the deaths of Othello and

Desdemona, and unsuccessful in that he fails to get away with the crime.

The idea of revenge, however, is not the most important driving force in the plot, even though the notion of justice recurs throughout. It might be more sensible to summarize a play that focuses so obsessively on love and sexual passion in terms of these forces. If the plot is the sum of causal events within the drama – a brief account of the way in which one thing leads to another – we would want to say that Iago's jealousy of both Othello and Cassio leads him to seek their downfall. He is joined in this enterprise by Roderigo, who is infatuated with Desdemona. Iago, possessed by an almost manic sexual mistrust of women, inspires a similar feeling in Othello, who becomes jealous in his turn. It is this jealousy that leads to the catastrophe, when Othello becomes convinced that his wife is an adulteress.

The important point to make here is that descriptions of the plot turn to a great extent on what is seen to be important in the action of the play and its sequence of events. Given that all plot synopses might be reduced to a formula, here we must say that Iago, seeking revenge, finds it through the sexual weaknesses of others. With this formula, further interpretation depends upon the elements of the description one wishes to stress: revenge, love or weakness. The whole question of plot interpretation is especially interesting and important in the case of *Othello*, in that it contains no developed sub-plot. Usually Shakespeare is inclined to vary the main story with one or more subsidiary story lines that offer diversity within the play, throwing light on each other and – crucially – on the main plot. In Othello the intrigue with Roderigo, Cassio's relationship with Bianca, and Emilia's with Iago, all have the possibility of being further developed, but they are not. Instead, everything in the play relates directly to the core: the interlocking relationships between Othello and Desdemona, and Othello and Iago. Significantly, none of the complications in the plot is 'real' – all are generated in the mind of Iago. Whereas an early Shakespeare play may be filled with incident – coincidences, muddled identities, twists in the story, and so on – here the basis of the action is starkly simple: Othello loves Desdemona and believes himself betrayed. Iago misleads him and all the other characters. This means that the interest of the play has little to do with physical action. What matter are the psychological, emotional and spiritual developments of the characters, their thoughts and feelings and responses, their inner life. In that sense the bare plot is merely a peg to hang more important issues on, and its simplicity heightens these other aspects.

There are, as usual in Shakespeare, inconsistencies in the play. Why is Roderigo tolerated by Desdemona in Act II, when we know that he had to be banished from her father's house for pursuing her? Why, indeed, is Roderigo introduced into the first part of Act II at all, when he doesn't speak? Is it not most unlikely that a chatterbox such as Emilia would not wonder why her husband should want a lady's embroidered handkerchief? And isn't the coincidence of so many people showing interest in that handkerchief — Iago, Emilia, Desdemona, Othello and Bianca all mention it — equally unbelievable? Can we really be expected to accept that Othello believes Desdemona has had the opportunity to commit adultery in the few hours they have been married? Can we credit that Othello would be convinced of this by a man he has already passed over for promotion, and who offers the flimsiest evidence, often couched in impertinent language?

The answer to all these questions is that so long as they do not undermine our basic confidence in the power and truthfulness of the play's important aspects, they do not matter. The plot, while it must work reasonably well, is only an instrument. We accept that this is fiction, not life, and that one kind of consistency has to be preferred to another.

There is one respect, however, in which this answer is not quite satisfactory, and in relation to which we do scrutinize the plot carefully. Of all Shakespeare's plays *Othello* is perhaps the most thoroughly ironic. *Irony* is discussed elsewhere in this study, but it must be mentioned here insofar as it issues from the plot itself. The plot of *Othello* is ironic in a number of respects First, it is clear that when characters seek to bring about the downfall of others, they succeed in destroying themselves: this is true of Iago, Othello and Roderigo. Second, the apparent motives for the plot — Othello's love for Desdemona, Iago's 'love' for Othello, Roderigo's love for Desdemona — turn into their opposites: hatred, lust and suspicion combine to drive on these characters and to entrap them. And even the actions of the minor characters are complicated by this ironic contradiction:

Emilia's love for her husband prevents her from acting on suspicion, and contributes to the catastrophe; Cassio's love for the general turns out to be a matter of getting back into his good graces to secure advancement; Bianca's love for Cassio is the infatuation of a professional prostitute, which plays its part in the plot mechanism. In each case the character's actions contribute to the final disaster: Emilia's silence, Bianca's nagging, Cassio's pleading. The third respect in which the plot generates irony is a matter of more detailed scrutiny: for the play is packed with lines rendered ironic by what has happened or what is to come. (For this, see the section on *Irony*). We are thus prepared to overlook the structural weaknesses of the plot because it contributes so effectively to the overall ironic import of the play. This can be observed more strikingly if we compare Shakespeare's treatment of the plot with the original from which he took it.

So far as we know, Shakespeare only invented one plot: the rest are taken from historical chronicles or from collections of French and Italian stories, popular in 16th-century England. In the case of *Othello*, the plot is lifted bodily from *The Moor of Venice* by one Geraldi Cinthio (1504–73) an Italian writer whose *Hecatommithi* (*The Hundred Tales*) existed in the original Italian and in a French translation – though Shakespeare's exact source is unknown and does not matter. What *are* of interest to readers and students are the differences and similarities between Shakespeare's approach to the plot, and Cinthio's, throwing light as they do on the playwright's workmanship and on the meaning of the play.

Source

In Cinthio's story the Ensign (Shakespeare's Iago) loves Disdemona (*sic*), the wife of a brave handsome Moor. When she fails to return his love it changes to hatred, and the Ensign determines that if he cannot possess Disdemona neither shall her husband. He sows suspicion and jealousy in the Moor's mind by a number of means, including the suggestion that Disdemona is having an affair with a captain (Shakespeare's Cassio). To prove this he leaves, in the captain's house, a handkerchief belonging to Disdemona. Finally the Ensign and the Moor together kill Disdemona and try to make her death look accidental. After this Cinthio's story has a number of complications that do not concern us: Shakespeare selected only the part of the narrative that suited his tragic purpose, and in so doing considerably altered the emphasis, both in plot and character relationships.

Treatment

The first thing to notice is how drastically Shakespeare simplified the story, and by so doing increased the tension. In Cinthio there is a great deal of plot detail; in *Othello* the emphasis is on the central relationships: Othello/Desdemona, Othello/Iago. In *The Moor of Venice* the narrative lasts over several weeks; Shakespeare shortens the action to about three days (excluding the trip between Venice and Cyprus).

Shakespeare simplifies the plot, but he makes the characters far more complex and more mysterious. In Cinthio the Moor appears as a kind of noble savage, unreflective and violent. Shakespeare's Othello is certainly capable of violence and prey to strong feelings but he is also broodingly introspective: his character contains tensions and contradictions and we witness considerable psychological development, especially in III, 3. On the other hand, by removing the motive of the Ensign's love for Disdemona, Shakespeare transforms his Iago from a man with a banal and specific grudge – jealousy – into a fascinating, inexplicable phenomenon over whose reasons for action there has been argument ever since. Where Cinthio records action Shakespeare analyses motive and feeling. His treatment of Othello is especially interesting in this respect. In Cinthio's version, for example, the Moor and the Ensign attempt to conceal the manner of Disdemona's death. Shakespeare retains a trace of this deceit in Othello's horrified denial to Emilia (V, 2, 128) but transforms it into an acute psychological and dramatic perception: the brave and frank Othello has been reduced to an evasive coward by the consequences of his own actions, which he cannot bear to face in the immediate aftermath. At this moment his image of himself is quite destroyed: naturally he acts out of character.

A comparison of Cinthio and Shakespeare also throws light on the playwright's method. For one thing, the difference between prose narrative and drama is a difference of economy: the playwright has limited time at his disposal, and little scope for detailed exposition. Thus Shakespeare's simplification of Cinthio's plot, so important to the dramatic intensity, is also a matter of practical theatre. Not only does Shakespeare simplify the material, he also compresses it; the final scene of the play telescopes several pages of incident in Cinthio. Where Cinthio is unpleasant but lacking in tension and pace Shakespeare moves the action forward, deepens the perspective and concentrates the dramatic impact for maximum effect.

Date

Othello was almost certainly written in the period of Shakespeare's career including the other great tragedies: *Hamlet, King Lear, Macbeth, Coriolanus,* and *Antony and Cleopatra.* This puts it in the first decade of the seventeenth century, and while there is little direct evidence for a particular year of composition, most subsequent scholars have agreed with the great 18th-century Shakespeare editor Malone that the play probably belongs to the years 1603–4.

Scene summaries, commentary, textual notes, and revision questions

Act I Scene 1

The play opens quietly, as if halfway through a scene. We eavesdrop on a conversation between Iago and Roderigo, a rich foolish Venetian who has been paying Iago for a service, the nature of which is at first unclear. It is night and they are near the house of Brabantio, Desdemona's father. When Iago tells Roderigo that the Moor (i.e. Othello) has married Desdemona against her father's will, they decide to rouse Brabantio and set him against Othello with the news. Brabantio, though a friend of Othello's, is already wary of him because of his swashbuckling character.

It then appears that Roderigo has been paying Iago to arrange a meeting for him with Desdemona: Roderigo is in love with the lady. Thus Roderigo now has a grudge against Othello for depriving him of Desdemona, while Iago also has a grudge against the general for promoting Cassio lieutenant over his head. They wake Brabantio and inflame his rage with the sexually suggestive language in which they convey the news of his daughter's marriage.

Commentary

This scene rapidly introduces the main material of the play: the themes of war and love; Othello's relationship with Desdemona; the atmosphere of treachery and sexual jealousy; and Iago's readiness to plot and lie in his own interest – a course of action he recommends to Roderigo. The scene also anticipates the central development of the plot, by establishing the idea of Iago's betrayal of Othello through the general's weakness for Desdemona. In theatrical terms the action moves vividly from the hushed conspiratorial tone of the opening to the painful, raucous crudity of Brabantio's awakening. Like much of the play, it takes place at night, and different night atmospheres are evoked: quiet, mysterious, dangerous. Like any good first scene it conveys such information about character, plot, situation and relationships as the audience need if they are to make sense of what follows but it does this obliquely. Our attention is first held by the mysterious conversation between Iago and Roderigo, and we have to work out what they are talking about. This draws us into the intimate tone in which much of the play is couched, despite its portrayal of a heroic central character. This is appropriate because that portrayal is concerned with the hero's inner life, not his external deeds.

Also present in this first scene are allusions to many of the images and motifs important in the play: the difference between appearance and reality; financial and military imagery; deceit; poisoning; animals and vermin; night; hell and devils – and above all, Iago's obsessive references to sexuality, which colour the whole play.

Tush, never tell me ... The first eighty-one lines of the play are mysterious. Othello is contemptuously referred to as 'he' and 'the Moor' but not named. It is made clear that he compares badly with Iago's portrait of himself as a plain honest man. Othello is presented as a rough bombastic boor. This part of the play is the first in a series of complex conversations between Iago and Roderigo that run through the work, forming a commentary on the main action – Roderigo's trust in Iago being an absurd and sometimes comic shadow of Othello's.

hast had my purse i.e. for interceding with Desdemona in his interest. However, it seems that Iago has taken the money and done nothing.

'Sblood God's blood – a common oath.

If ever I did dream ... Notice the crudeness with which Iago makes a fool of Roderigo, protesting his innocence in the face of the facts.

Oft capp'd Taken off their caps, i.e. they showed respect.

Nonsuits my mediators Doesn't accept the advice of Iago's supporters.

'Certes' Certainly.

arithmetician Calculator. Iago here implies that Cassio is more of a theoretical than a practical man. He develops this theme in the next few lines.

damn'd in a fair wife According to the Italian proverb, a man with a pretty wife is damned – because of the way she attracts other men. This sour comment ironically foreshadows the play's theme of sexual betrayal.

a squadron A formed body of troops.

bookish theoric Learned theory. Iago develops the theme of the 'arithmetician'.

toged consuls In ancient Rome those unsuited to war – counsellors and the elderly – wore togas: flowing robes restricted to men of high rank.

propose Explain or discuss.

his eyes had seen the proof Othello has seen Iago perform bravely in battle. The implication is that Othello should therefore prefer Iago to Cassio.

Rhodes An island in the Aegean sea.

lee'd, and calm'd In the lee – i.e. the shelter – of another ship.

debitor and creditor One who keeps accounts.

counter-caster One who counts with an abacus – i.e. a calculating frame with balls sliding on wires. This is another contemptuous reference to Cassio as a clerk. Their frequency indicates the depth of Iago's bitterness.

God bless the mark A common oath, here used sarcastically.

ancient The word is a corruption of 'ensign' – which is Iago's rank, making him junior to Cassio.

curse of service i.e. this is what happens when you do your duty: you are overlooked.

Preferment goes by letter and affection Promotion depends on recommendation and personal liking – not on seniority, as it should.

gradation Seniority.

each second/Stood heir to the first Each subordinate was in line for the job above.

affin'd Bound.

knee-crooking Bowing. This speech is a typical outburst in which Iago witheringly dismisses the fools who merely do as they are told, instead of looking to their own interests.

doting ... bondage Fooled into obedience by respect.

Whip me I care nothing for.

trimm'd in forms and visages Equipped with the outward appearance.

I would not be Iago ... From here to line 65 notice the appearances of the 'hidden identity' theme. Having said at line 11 that he knows his own worth, Iago here announces his deception of Othello.

peculiar Private.

figure Shape.

complement extern External appearance. The distinction between what is and what seems to be recurs again and again through the play.

I will wear ... This has become proverbial. Here it anticipates the ironic appellation of Iago as 'honest'. Iago is saying that on the day when he shows his true intentions, he'll expose even his heart for doves to peck. Compare this attitude to honesty and to emotion with Othello's and Desdemona's. They both advocate and practise openness – until Othello is corrupted by Iago.

I am not what I am This paradox enshrines an ironic truth about Iago. He is not what he seems to others, nor is he what he seems to himself.

thicklips A patronizing reference to Othello's negroid appearance.

Plague him with flies Infect his reputation with innuendo.

changes of vexation Suggestive hints. Roderigo is urged to do Iago's dirty work for him.

colour Justification.

timorous Frightening.

bags Money-bags.

Zounds God's wounds (an oath).

tupping Making love to. The reference to the ram proverbially suggests excessive lust.

snorting Snoring. Notice the deliberate crudeness of Iago's language in these exchanges. He wishes to make Othello's relationship with Desdemona appear merely bestial.

distempering draughts Stimulating drinks.

start Startle.

grange Isolated farmhouse.

cover'd with a Barbary horse Copulating with an Arab stallion.

nephews Grandsons.

coursers for cousins and gennets for germans Horses for blood-relations. This, in Iago's vulgar joke, is what will result from the union of the 'mare' Desdemona with the 'stallion' Othello.

the beast with two backs Two people involved in sexual intercourse. Again love is reduced to lust.

odd-even and dull watch Midnight.

your allowance With your permission.

wit Intellect.

extravagant and wheeling Roderigo implies here that Othello is feckless, rootless and therefore untrustworthy. 'Wheeling' means 'wandering'.

my dream . . . It seems Brabantio has had a premonition of what is to come. This is echoed much later in his daughter's premonition of death, Act IV Scene 3.

wholesome Suitable.

loud reason General approval.

stands in act In progress.

fathom Degree of ability.

flag Indication. Iago is quite frank here about his dishonesty.

Sagittar Probably an inn.

O unhappy girl! . . . Notice Brabantio's extreme distress. Not only only has his daughter eloped, but she has gone off with an outsider.

treason of the blood This is ambiguous. It can refer either to Desdemona's 'disloyalty' to her father or to her supposed lustfulness.

property Nature.

deserve Reward.

Act I Scene 2

Iago enters with Othello, whom we see for the first time. Assuming his role as the loyal Lieutenant, Iago warns Othello of Brabantio's anger. As they talk, Cassio arrives with an urgent summons from the duke: Othello is to attend the council of state at once. Then Brabantio enters, denouncing Othello for using

witchcraft to seduce his daughter, and insisting that the case be
brought before the council now in session.

Commentary

Notice how Iago speaks first in this scene, though Othello is the
hero, suggesting at once his quiet dominance of the general,
whom he tries to alarm by speaking of Brabantio's rage.
Immediately the contrast between Iago's insinuating character
and Othello's open one is established – a contrast that is maintained and intensified throughout the play. In the same straightforward way Othello faces Brabantio's charges of witchcraft. In
sharp contrast to Iago's description of him in the previous scene
as awkward and pompous, his language shows him to be calm,
dignified, incisive and authoritative. When Iago and Roderigo
draw swords, Othello instinctively takes control of the situation
and subdues them. While advancing the action, the scene is
notable for the understated way in which the hero is introduced,
conversing with Iago. On the other hand, his colour naturally
marks him out from the other characters.

very stuff of conscience Basic principles.
I lack iniquity I am not sufficiently dishonest. Paradoxically, this
  statement itself could hardly be more dishonest. It shows Iago's
  cynicism, and hints, too, at his enjoyment of the situation. Compare his
  protestation of innocence in the opening lines of the play.
yerk'd Stabbed.
prated Babbled. Iago is referring to Brabantio here, and trying to stir
  up Othello against him.
I did full hard forbear him I just managed to put up with him.
magnifico One of the rulers of Venice.
As double as As influential as. In Venice the duke was only the first
  among equals.
grievance Penalty.
cable Scope.
signiory Ruling council. Observe Othello's pride of birth in this
  speech.
know Be known.
provulgate Announce.
seige Rank.
demerits Merits.
unbonneted As an equal. When everyone wore hats, removing the hat
  was a sign of respect.
unhoused Wandering. Note how Othello agrees with Roderigo's

description of him at I, 1, 136. The play constantly emphasizes Othello's status as an outsider.

raised Alarmed or roused.

parts Qualities.

perfect Prepared. Unlike Iago, Othello is transparently honest.

Janus Roman god of entrances and exits, thus facing both ways. By extension the word implies two-faced, which is an apt oath for the double-dealing Iago.

some heat Urgency.

several Separate.

carrack A treasure ship. Iago's crude reference to Desdemona – 'boarded' – has implications of both capture and sexual possession.

To who? . . . It later transpires that Cassio already knows. He is loyally keeping what he supposes to be a secret.

Marry An oath, diminutive of 'By the Virgin Mary'. The teasing pun here is obvious and typical.

You, Roderigo . . . Iago at once displays his apparent zeal on Othello's behalf, and his desire to protect from others a man who is paying him well.

refer me Lay my case before.

things of sense All right-thinking people. Brabantio emphasizes his belief that no normal Venetian girl would willingly love a Moor.

her guardage . . . Brabantio here refers to himself as Desdemona's rightful guardian. When married she will pass to the guardianship of her husband.

gross in sense Obvious.

practis'd i.e. witchcraft.

weakens motion Sedates or tranquillizes.

inhibited Prohibited.

out of warrant Illegal. Brabantio's whole speech makes a point fundamental to the play: the strangeness of the union between Desdemona and Othello. We must grasp this if we are to understand Othello's peculiar susceptibility to Iago's insinuations. He shows himself aware of his suspect status in Venice – admired and tolerated but not accepted. Eventually Desdemona comes to represent for him not only his passionate love but also the untrustworthiness of Venetian society, of which he has never been a full part.

course of direct session Due process of law.

Act I Scene 3

The duke and senators receive news and discuss it: two Turkish fleets have combined to invade Cyprus, a Venetian territory towards which they are now sailing. Othello enters the council chamber with Brabantio, Cassio, Iago and Roderigo. The duke commissions him to lead the battle against the Turks, but is interrupted by Brabantio's account of Desdemona's seduction. Othello admits his marriage with Brabantio's daughter, asserting that she entered into it of her own free will. When Brabantio challenges this, asserting witchcraft, Othello sends Iago to fetch Desdemona – on the duke's orders – so that she may tell her own story.

While they wait, Othello explains to the council how he and his wife fell in love. When Desdemona arrives, she confirms this account, supplying further detail. Brabantio grudgingly agrees to accept the marriage. Othello is then formally appointed general, and Desdemona's request to be allowed to accompany him is granted. Othello directs Iago to bring her to him later with Iago's wife Emilia as her attendant. The duke then orders Othello to leave for Cyprus at once, and the scene ends with a long complex conversation between Iago and Roderigo in which the disconsolate Roderigo is comforted by Iago, who explains his own cynical and opportunist attitude to life. This variation on the theme of 'every man for himself' contrasts sharply with the exhibition of passionate love between Othello and Desdemona that we have just witnessed. Assuring him that this marriage cannot last, Iago bids Roderigo bide his time and trust in Iago. When Roderigo leaves, Iago's contempt for him bursts out as he formulates the next stage of his plot to displace Cassio, dupe Roderigo and revenge himself on Othello and Desdemona.

Commentary

Central to this scene is the juxtaposition of love and war, common in Shakespeare's plays, and made especially dramatic here by the way in which Brabantio interrupts the council with his complaint. We see Othello both as supreme commander and devoted husband; Desdemona as the adoring wife who discovered love through admiration of her husband's feats of courage, suffering and endurance. Again and again through the scene the urgency of repelling the Turkish attack takes second place to the love of Othello and Desdemona. This helps to provide the heroic scale – necessary for tragedy – on which the development of their love and its disastrous outcome takes place. In contrast, Iago's long talk with Roderigo – one of several throughout the play – makes clear the spiteful pettiness of his nature and, in particular, his inability to admit the possibility of a generous love. Othello and Iago both talk about sexual desire, but whereas Othello allots to it its legitimate place within marriage, Iago concludes it to be invariably treacherous and dishonest – like himself.

composition Agreement.

jump Agree.

aim Guess.

Nay ... fearful sense The duke means that it is possible to make a judgement on the basis of the information. The inconsistencies of the reports do not obscure the main point – that the Turkish fleet is making for Cyprus.

by About.

assay of reason Reasonable test.

pageant Decoy.

keep us in false gaze Fool us.

with more facile ... bear it Win it more easily.

brace State of defence.

dress'd in Equipped with.

wake and wage Start and carry on. The senator is explaining that because Cyprus is both more desirable to the Turks, and more vulnerable for the Venetians, their attack on Rhodes must be a ploy to distract Venetian attention.

Ottomites Turks. The Turkish empire was ruled by the Ottoman (or Ottomite) dynasty.

injointed United.

re-stem Steer again.

free duty Deepest respect.

recommends Informs.

Ottoman See 'Ottomites' above.

flood-gate Overwhelming.

it is still itself Nothing makes any difference to it. Notice how Othello's personal affairs not only break into this vital discussion about national security, but even displace it for a while.

mountebanks Quacks.

sans Without (from the French).

read ... sense Interpret in the severest way.

our proper son Our own son (royal plural).

Stood in Was exposed to.

head and front Extent and appearance.

set Soft. Just as Iago is fond of contrasting his own straightforwardness with other men's deviousness or excessive theory, so Othello likes to set apart his plain speaking from the sophisticated ways of the Venetian aristocracy. This is shown to have been crucial in attracting Desdemona to him, as she testifies in I, 3, 252.

pith Strength.

dearest Most extreme.

broil Fighting.

a round unvarnish'd tale ... While by no means a flowery speaker, Othello reveals a talent for eloquence which contradicts his disclaimers. Only at the height of his jealousy (IV. 1, 43) does he become literally speechless.

I won his daughter The blunt final phrase is typical, as though Othello, embarrassed at his own eloquence, needs to finish abruptly.

her motion/Blush'd at her self Brabantio insists on Desdemona's shyness. This phrase seems to mean that she blushed even at her own movements, because they attracted attention to her. This shyness reminds us what a mighty step it is for her to elope – and with Othello!

rules of nature ... Iago has already hinted that the marriage is unnatural with his crude animal similes. Later in the play he manages to convince Othello himself that this is the case.

vouch Claim.

overt Open.

thin habits Flimsy appearances. (Habits meant, and can still mean, clothes.)

poor likelihoods Unlikely assumptions.

modern seemings Trivial appearances.

prefer Charge.

Sagittar This is presumed to be an inn.

Her father ... Brabantio was a friend until Othello married his daughter. This again illustrates Othello's precarious position in Venetian society.

antres Caves.

idle Empty.

hint Occasion.

process Custom.

Anthropophagi Another word for 'cannibals'.

Devour up my discourse This is proof, if it were needed, that Othello can speak compellingly.

pliant Convenient.

by parcel In part.

intentively As a whole.

beguile Draw forth.

She swore ... woo her Notice Othello's tender evocation of Desdemona's emotion, which in turn moves him – a beautiful example of his capacity for delicate feeling.

This only is the witchcraft Othello means to say that his witchcraft is the simple truth, but this speech is in itself a tribute to the power of eloquence and a complete refutation of Iago's crude innuendo. Desdemona's love is based not on lust but on admiration and the sense that Othello embodies the masculine virtues of courage, endurance and daring. He also appears exotic in her eyes by virtue of his travels, his deeds and his person.

Men do Men make the best of what they have. An amiable if limited character, the duke is fond of stating the obvious. He represents within the play the ordinary Venetian grandee as opposed to Othello's extraordinary character.

Where most you owe obedience This phrase echoes the scene in *King Lear* when Cordelia, Lear's daughter, is forced to choose between her husband and her father.

a divided duty Desdemona acknowledges her duty to her father, but tries to persuade him that she regards Othello as her mother regarded Brabantio.

God bu'y God be with you.

To hang clogs on'em To restrain them.

sentence Proverbial or wise saying.

grise Degree.

When remedies Notice the lapse into rhyming couplets, common in Shakespeare to suggest impersonal, proverbial wisdom, or – as in this case – banal commonplaces. The sense here is exactly expressible in the saying: it's no use crying over spilt milk.

So let the Turk . . . Brabantio sarcastically echoes the duke's couplets, replying in the sense of another saying: fine words butter no parsnips. In doing so he foreshadows the association of Othello's victories in love and in war (see Act I, Scenes 1 and 2)

beguile i.e. deprive by means of guile and deception.

Beseech you now Brabantio impatiently turns back to the matter of the Turkish invasion.

fortitude Power of resistance.

a substitute . . . voice on you Montano, the commander in Cyprus, is a competent general but public opinion, to which we must bow, would feel more secure with Othello in charge. Once again the duke shows himself to be a man of too many words.

slubber Besmear.

new fortunes . . . It is ambiguous whether the duke refers to Othello's earlier successes or to his marriage. The latter seems likely: a contrast between the pain and heroism of war and the quiet happiness of domestic life, is commonplace in Shakespeare.

thrice-driven Winnowed three times.

agnize Acknowledge.

alacrity Eagerness.

fit disposition Suitable provision.

reference of place Regard for her position i.e. as my wife and a senator's daughter.

exhibition Maintenance. In this formal passage Othello is proudly asking that his wife be looked after as befits her station and birth. This is an implied compliment to Brabantio, but also alludes to the doctrine, fundamental in all Shakespeare's plays, that there is a proper social order, which reflects the universal order and which should be observed in all things – such as the appropriate treatment of the commander's wife.

impatient thoughts Free of Othello's pride, Desdemona shows her
  mildness and good judgment here.
unfolding Explanation.
charter in your voice Permission through your support.
downright violence Elopement in the face of family and public
  opinion.
scorn of fortunes Neglect of the consequences.
utmost pleasure Most extreme demand.
visage in his mind Desdemona means that the noble qualities she saw
  in Othello's face were confirmed when she got to know his mind.
A moth of peace An idler. The moth is seen here as a creature without
  use. A moth of *peace* because Othello is going to war and she does not
  want to be left behind.
rites i.e. the rites of marriage, including sexual intercourse. In this
  speech Desdemona's frankness about sexual relations appears to
  contradict her father's description of her shyness, but in fact confirms
  it: what Desdemona lacks is prurience, or the overheated imaginings
  about sex Othello himself later displays. Brabantio has earlier
  overstated his daughter's shyness to strengthen his charge of
  witchcraft against Othello.
dear This may be a pun: in Elizabethan English 'dear' can mean
  extreme. Here the word can signify both prolonged and beloved.
Nor to . . . satisfaction The meaning of these lines is unclear. Othello
  seems to be saying that his desire for Desdemona's company springs
  from a wish for *mental* intercourse with his wife, not from sexual
  passion, which would partly contradict what she has just said. On the
  other hand, he makes the point that he is too old to be dominated by
  mere passion, implying, like her, that carnal, mental and spiritual
  needs must be satisfied in marriage. The passage is important in the
  light of Othello's later suspicions: it indicates the passionately physical
  nature of their love, but also how it transcends mere appetite,
  involving their whole natures and thus being raised to the tragic level.
scant Neglect.
when light-wing'd toys If trifles.
feather'd Cupid The Roman god of love who shot his feathered arrows
  into the hearts of men. 'Feather'd' may also be a pun on Cupid's wings.
foils Befuddles.
speculative and active instruments Thoughts and senses. Cupid's
  arrows cause men to go more or less mad with love.
disports Pleasures.
skillet Saucepan.
indign Unworthy.
head Opposition.
quality or respect rank.
honesty . . . The first time the word, persistently associated with Iago, is
  used in this sense. Notice its many recurrences through the play, as it
  takes on an intensifying irony.

Look to her . . . Brabantio's couplet anticipates a point Iago later uses against Desdemona. If she has deceived one man, how can she be trusted?

My life upon her faith . . . This remark becomes retrospectively ironic because it is Othello's unjust suspicion of her faith that precipitates the tragedy.

honest Iago The scene is full of painful ironies. Using the epithet noted above, here Othello consigns Desdemona to the care of the man he should most mistrust.

noble heart . . . Notice Iago's inveterately sarcastic treatment of Roderigo. The audience know his real feelings: Roderigo does not.

incontinently Immediately.

death is our physician . . . Ironic pathos arises from the fact that Roderigo confides such thoughts to Iago who is apparently his 'physician' but actually the cause of his death.

guinea-hen i.e. a woman. Iago here begins the most comprehensive explanation of his cynicism. He impresses and patronizes Roderigo while saying what he really thinks he believes.

fond Foolish.

a fig! Nonsense. Propounding the common doctrine of Shakespearian villains, Iago explains that life is all a matter of getting your own way by ruthlessness and will-power.

gender Kind, type, genus.

reason Iago describes reason as that faculty with which we control the baser passions and balance them. This contradicts a prevailing view in Shakespeare's time, which saw reason as a God-given and supreme faculty, not for restraining base passions but for bringing order to legitimate ones, i.e. love, proper pride etc. The twisting of true doctrines is typical of Iago's plausibility.

unbitted Uncontrolled (as of a horse).

sect, or scion Both words mean 'cutting' – in the horticultural sense.

perdurable Everlasting.

stead Help.

Put money in thy purse Besides the obvious meaning – and we should remember that Iago has been doing well financially out of Roderigo – this phrase takes on the sense of 'be in readiness' and 'look after your own interests'.

defeat thy favour Disguise your face.

answerable sequestration A similar end to it.

changeable Iago plays on the theme of woman's fickleness to both Othello and Roderigo. His views are sharply contrasted with Desdemona's actual behaviour.

locusts A kind of sweet fruit.

acerb Bitter.

coloquintida Bitter apple.

When she is sated . . . Notice how Iago's obsession with Desdemona's sexuality makes his plans turn on it. This is not just a tragic love-story:

the power and unpredictability of sexual attraction are central to the play.

sanctimony Holiness.

a frail vow i.e. the marriage vow.

super-subtle Exquisite. Iago harps on the contrast between the delicate white Desdemona and the virile black Othello.

hang'd An obscene pun. Hanged men are supposed to experience orgasm at the moment of death. Roderigo runs the risk of death for committing adultery.

Thou art sure of me Characteristic irony: Iago knows that the opposite is the case.

my cause is hearted I'm completely committed to my cause.

be communicative Make common cause.

cuckold him Commit adultery with his wife.

There are many... Ironic. There are more events than Iago himself suspects.

Traverse Off you go.

betimes Early.

Thus do I... Notice the crucial change here from prose to verse. Each of Iago's lengthy prose conversations with Roderigo is followed or preceded by a verse soliloquy. Each time there is also a change of mood: the conversations are broad, racy, allusive and even comical, using a colloquial style and a falsely intimate tone. In the soliloquies, Iago expresses what purport to be his inmost thoughts in the quieter, intenser verse form.

my fool my purse A piece of word-play apt to Iago's cynical discourse and his superficial cleverness.

snipe Fool.

But for my sport... Notice the rapid changes of tone in this soliloquy, from flippant patronage to hatred. The black humour of the prose conversation is absent.

He's done my office i.e. made love to my wife. Observe how Iago characterizes the others – Cassio, Othello, Roderigo, Desdemona – in terms of their sexual roles as he sees them; nothing else matters.

Will do, as if for surety Act as if it were true. Not only does Iago involve others in lies and half-truths: he acts on them himself.

proper Handsome and virile.

how, how... Far from being a far-seeing strategist, Iago is shown in this passage to be stumbling from one expedient to another.

abuse Misuse, i.e. fill with lies.

He i.e. Cassio.

dispose Manner.

led by the nose Made a fool of.

Revision questions on Act I

1 What role does Roderigo play in the first Act?
2 How is Othello's entry prepared for and in what character does he first come on stage?
3 What reasons do Othello and Desdemona give for their love and marriage?
4 How does Shakespeare convey necessary information to the audience throughout the Act?

Act II Scene 1

The action moves to Cyprus, where the Turkish fleet has been destroyed by a storm. Bad weather has also dispersed the Venetian ships; first Cassio, then Iago with Desdemona, then Othello come ashore. As usual in Shakespeare, the storm takes on a symbolic meaning, here ironic: appearing at first to signify the storm of battle, which will clear; in retrospect it portends the conflict to emerge from the very heart of Othello's success in love and war as foreshadowed in the previous scene. If the elements appear to be on his side this time, destroying the Turkish fleet, that good fortune only heightens the pathos when disaster appears. Othello, like other Shakespearian tragic heroes, is a hitherto successful man whose luck deserts him at a critical time.

While they wait for Othello, Desdemona and Iago have the kind of superficial, witty conversation familiar in Shakespeare's early comedies: a mixture of banter and flirtation. Here the dialogue takes on an ominous significance from the contrast of Iago's vulgar innuendoes with Desdemona's playfulness. When Othello enters there is a striking change of mood and tone from worldly wit to lyrical grandeur.

As in Act I Scene 3, the scene concludes with a lengthy exchange between Iago and Roderigo. Iago raises Roderigo's hopes with the lie that Desdemona loves Cassio, suggesting that she will transfer her love to Roderigo when Cassio is safely out of the way. Roderigo does not notice the contemptuous estimate this view suggests of both Desdemona's sexual conduct and his own discrimination. In his closing soliloquy Iago makes this contempt explicit, and explains his own motive for revenge: the belief in Othello's adultery with Emilia. Iago's perverseness is here made evident: he is determined to believe the rumours about his wife, however slender the evidence and against the grain of what he knows about Othello.

Commentary

In this scene we become aware of the way in which Shakespeare exploits minor characters, Montano for example, to highlight the leading characters, provide a background for them and carry the action along. They also serve another function crucial for the audience: they provide both a frame for the protagonists – the sense that there is a world outside their immediate concerns – and a context of 'ordinary life' within which to evaluate the extraordinary life of Othello, Desdemona and Iago. Look, for example, at the way in which Montano and the Third Gentleman discuss Cassio's affairs (lines 25–33). The physical world too is brought before us: ships; the sea; the storm. This is done, as always in Shakespeare, entirely in the language, there being only minimal scenery in the theatre of his time. The sea is especially important, entering into the symbolic texture of the play. When, for instance, Othello says 'If after every tempest come such calmness' (II, 1, 185), this ironically foreshadows the tragic fact that after the crucial tempest of his own life – his suspicion and murder of his wife – the only calmness will be death.

main Sea.
ha'ruffian'd so Been so destructive.
hold the mortise Stand up straight.
segregation i.e. scattering.
banning shore i.e. the shore is the only thing holding back these high seas.
burning bear A star. So high is the sea it seems to reach the stars.
guards Stars in the constellation of the Burning Bear.
pole The Pole star. This occupies a constant place in the sky, and sailors used it to steer by.
enchafed Angry.
embay'd Sailed into port.
designment Plan.
wrack and sufferance Both words mean 'damage'.
Veronesa A kind of ship, probably a cutter.

in full commission With full authority.

sadly Worried. Cassio's anxiety for Othello's safety is evident.

Even till . . . regard Until the sea and sky are blurred with looking at them.

bark Boat.

approv'd allowance Demonstrated capability.

my hopes . . . cure My hopes are sustained by not being excessive. Excessive hope leads quickly to its opposite.

brow i.e. edge.

shot of courtesy Salute with cannon-fire.

achiev'd Won. Notice Cassio's very flowery speech.

paragons Exceeds.

quirks of blazoning pens Extravagant praises of writers. Shakespeare is fond of such little digs at his own profession, but he's also making a serious point about Desdemona's very special quality.

the essential vesture of creation Her natural state.

Does bear all excellency Has every virtue. Cassio's praise is just as extravagant as any writer's.

gutter'd Submerged. Like the congregated sands, these are dangers to the sailor.

ensteep'd Under water.

having sense of beauty The notion here – that even the rocks and elements recognise Desdemona's beauty – is an example of the pathetic fallacy: the reflection of human characteristics in the non-human world. It is hyperbolic in just the sense dismissed by Cassio at line 63 above.

captain's captain These words are echoed by Iago when he says of Desdemona: 'the general's wife is now the general.'

conduct Safe-keeping.

footing Landing.

A se'nnight's speed By a week.

Jove King of the gods in Roman mythology.

extincted Extinguished.

riches i.e. Desdemona.

let her have your knees Kneel.

Enwheel thee round Surround you. Cassio is really carried away. As his later attempts to retrieve his reputation show, he is somewhat weak-headed, and not altogether unworthy of Iago's contempt.

gall i.e. spoil.

extend Stretch out, i.e. to the extent of kissing Emilia.

Sir, would she . . . This speech is a good example of how Iago too can be courtly when he wishes.

I find it, I I'm the one who has to listen to her talk. Iago's humour is an example of the many references in the play to the characteristic ways of men and of women. Compare IV, 3, 84–105.

ha'list Desire. Here Iago presents himself as the humorously long-suffering husband.

chides with thinking Thinks her reproaches rather than speaking them.

you ha' ... Emilia takes up the joke.

pictures out o' doors Wearing make-up, i.e. not what they seem.

Bells Bells, like women, have tongues. They talk too much, Iago implies.

Players in your ... beds Iago is coining cheap paradoxes: women are never what you expect them to be. He says that women treat their work superficially but take their sexual pleasures seriously. Note that Iago's personal venom is barely veiled by the humour here.

You shall not Emilia enters ironically into the spirit of the exchange.

there's one gone ... In the midst of the banter Desdemona asks anxiously after her husband. Here we see wifely concern conflicting with what she apparently feels to be her duty of sustaining a relaxed manner in the role of the commander's wife in her first public appearance.

I am not ... otherwise A curious echo of Iago's words at I, 1, 65. Desdemona tacitly admits to the fears under her frivolous manner.

birdlime A gluey substance put on trees to catch birds. An ironic hint of Iago's role in relation to Desdemona.

frieze A coarse woollen cloth.

If she be fair ... Making riddles is common in the lighter parts of Shakespeare's plays.

Fair Means both 'beautiful' and 'blond'.

wit More than verbal cleverness: aptness or acuteness.

black Dark-haired or dark-complexioned.

folly Both foolishness and sexual licence. The whole passage turns on a series of such puns and double meanings.

There's none so foul ... do All women, whatever their personal qualities, indulge in lewdness.

justly put on ... itself Won the praise even of malicious people.

To change ... tail Exchange one triviality for another. There is also a lewd meaning depending on the equivalence of 'tail' with thighs.

To suckle fools For bearing children and making small-talk.

liberal Licentious.

He takes her ... Notice the abrupt change from levity to malevolence in Iago's aside, though the subject-matter – lust – is the same.

whisper Whipper-snapper.

I will catch you ... Iago develops the theme of himself as the spider.

kiss'd your three fingers Kissing his own hand was a common form of greeting from a man to a woman. Iago dwells on this lasciviously.

clyster-pipes Again the sexual innuendo: these are tubes for washing the vagina.

warrior Othello greets his wife as a comrade.

It gives me wonder ... Another change of tone from menace to regal grandeur is announced by the trumpet.

As hell's As far as hell is.

Succeeds in unknown fate Can come in the unknown future. A sadly true prediction:

forbid/But Allow.

set down the pegs i.e. untune the instrument by loosening the pegs which hold the strings.

As honest as I am Iago's laconic allusion to his own reputation with Othello.

well desir'd Popular, well-liked.

prattle out of fashion Chatter in an uncharacteristic way.

coffers Luggage.

challenge Require.

court of guard Guardroom.

thus i.e. on your lips.

with what violence See I, 3, 345.

act of sport Sexual intercourse. Iago here shows his skill in apparently commonsense reasoning. With Roderigo as with Othello, he is always ready with reasons and there is never time for his interlocutor to examine their speciousness.

abus'd Disappointed.

heave the gorge Feel disgusted.

disrelish No longer attracted to.

pregnant Evident.

position Supposition.

conscionable Ruled by conscience.

salt Lecherous.

stamp Counterfeit.

condition Character.

Blest fig's-end! Nonsense.

the wine she drinks i.e. she has normal appetites.

paddle Stroke, play.

incorporate Implied, inevitable.

tainting Criticising.

qualification Satisfaction.

apt and of great credit Appropriate and creditable. Iago is sneering ironically. As so often, he says more than he means.

The Moor . . . husband Iago acknowledges Othello's virtues and this inflames him the more.

absolute lust . . . There is something horrible about this echo of Othello's words (I, 3, 264). Iago adds revenge to lust as a cause of love.

diet Satisfy.

the lustful Moor See note on I, 3, 385.

Or failing so . . . Notice Iago's uncertainty about the outcome of his plot.

I trash I check.

putting on Investigation.

in the rank garb As loose living.

Cassio . . . The little justification for Iago's suspicion of Cassio and

Othello suggests either paranoia, or sexual obsession; or the search for
a sufficient motive for his plot, beyond mere hatred.

egregiously Surpassingly.

practising Plotting.

Even to madness . . . Notice the conventional couplet ending and the
banal pointing of the moral. The last line seems tacked on for effect.
Yet it is fitting that Iago should give voice to his own situation.

Act II Scene 2

This very brief scene provides a vantage point outside the main
action for observing Othello at the high point of his career. It
hints at the pathetic contrast between his confidence as expressed in the proclamation and the undermining of his position
that we know to be in progress from earlier scenes.

Commentary

The juxtaposition of legitimate pride (spoken) and the uncertainty of human prosperity (unspoken) is indicated without comment, but by context. This is typical of Shakespeare's ability to
say something without stating it, and forms part of the justification for such short scenes, which also, of course, help to carry
forward the action.

mere perdition Utter destruction.

offices Servants' quarters. Servants were usually confined to the house
at night.

told Struck.

Act II Scene 3

Having given directions to the guard, Othello goes off with
Desdemona. Cassio admits to Iago that he has a weak head; Iago
manages to make him drunk and quarrelsome, having already
done the same to Roderigo and three Cypriots. Iago's plan
works: Roderigo provokes Cassio and they fight, raising a din
that brings Othello out to see what the matter is. By appearing to
defend Cassio, Iago puts the blame for the fight on him, and
Cassio is dismissed from office by Othello, who is all the more
angry because (a) he has given special orders to his soldiers
against rowdiness, despite the celebrations, and (b) the fight has

interrupted his first hours alone with Desdemona. Once again the authority of his voice is apparent: he will brook no disobedience, however slight. Othello leaves and Iago pretends to befriend Cassio, urging him to ask for Desdemona's intercession with her husband. Cassio agrees to do this and leaves.

Again the scene ends with exchanges between Roderigo and Iago, this time prefaced by a soliloquy in which the Ensign explains how he is going to persuade Othello that Desdemona's pleading for Cassio can only mean that she loves him. Iago plans to use Emilia to ask for Desdemona's help — thus unwittingly planting the seed not of Cassio's ultimate downfall but his own.

Commentary

The comic and burlesque strain of the play emerges in this scene, albeit coloured with the sinister presence of Iago, who generates a false air of good fellowship to encourage drunkenness in his fellows. That Iago is aware of the comedy and takes a dark satisfaction in it is apparent from his soliloquy (II, 3, 44–57). The drinking scene and the songs are familiar elements in other Shakespeare plays, providing in themselves a broad humour besides allowing us to observe characters under different, more relaxed conditions; also forging a crucial link in the chain of the plot by decisively putting Cassio out of the general's favour. Notice on what small details that plot is built: a drunken brawl, mistaken appearances, a lost handkerchief etc. The triviality of these incidents intensifies the pathos, rather than diminishing it, by showing the fragility of human life. It also shows up the absurdity of Iago's pretensions to grand plotting.

the honourable stop To do no more than is honourable
to outsport discretion To go too far in revelling. Othello's use of the
  word here contrasts with Iago's rather different use of 'sport' below, at
  II, 3, 16.
with my personal eye In person. Cassio fusses to please Othello.
honest . . . Any mention of Iago's name seems to bring forth this
  epithet from Othello, who has a dangerously fixed idea about it. This
  fixed idea plays its part in blinding him to any faint suspicion later that
  Iago may be deliberately deceiving him.
with your earliest As soon as you are up.
profit Pleasure.

Not this hour Not for an hour.

cast Left.

exquisite lady . . . game Notice the persistent contrast between Iago's suggestive comments on Desdemona and Cassio's respectful ones.

a parley of provocation An invitation, i.e. to love.

stoup Four pint jar.

black Othello Iago can rarely bring himself to name the general without some periphrasis or qualification.

craftily qualified Carefully diluted.

Now my sick fool . . . Here we witness Iago in the act of working out his plan.

carous'd/Potations Drunk draughts of wine.

pottle-deep To the bottom of the bottle.

hold their honour . . . distance Sensitive to any insult, however slight or imagined.

The very elements The absolute dregs.

rouse Deep drink.

cannikin . . . soldier drunk A typical drinking song.

potting Drinking. Shakespeare is fond of making jokes about his countrymen being drunkards and madmen.

swag-bellied Pot-bellied.

Almain German.

King Stephen . . . about thee This is part of a popular Elizabethan ballad. Songs are an integral part of most Shakespeare plays, witness to the popular entertainments and the courtly dramas to which his work owes so much, and which both feature music. In this scene the atmosphere is deceptively lightened before the violence which foreshadows the tragedy's culmination. In fact the drunkenness itself contains an element of crude violence never far below the surface in this play with its ambience of war, intrigue and the soldier's life.

exquisite . . . Cassio is well and truly drunk.

odd Casual.

horologue . . . set Twice round the clock. Iago is preparing the ground for Cassio's disgrace by suggesting his undependability, drunk or sober.

ingraft Ingrained.

infirmity The second use of this word. See above, II, 3, 120.

mazzard head.

Diablo The devil.

carve Choose.

propriety Normal state, i.e. of peacefulness.

In quarter On good terms.

Devesting Undressing.

some planet The planets and their movements were thought to influence human life for good or ill.

odds Quarrel. Iago does his usual trick of making the guilt of others more evident by appearing to defend them. In this scene he is going to add Cassio to his list of dupes.

wisest censure Maturest judgment.

unlace Cast off.

to danger Dangerously.

blood Anger. Here we observe Othello's natural authority in action, but also his quick temper and violent passions, which bode ill for the future. In this speech he puts what he sees as his public duty above any personal affection. When killing Desdemona he persuades himself it is for the same reason.

safer guides Reason.

collied Made dark.

rout Quarrel.

approv'd Proved guilty.

town of war Fortified town. Othello insists that his men set a good example of calm to the citizens.

court Guardroom.

partially affin'd . . . office Prejudiced by any connection.

near i.e. strictly.

I had rather . . . Iago briefly damns Cassio by defending him.

might see Have seen.

pass Ignore. Iago returns to his act of the simple, sensible soldier.

recover Regain the esteem of. Iago is as good at seeing the bright side for Cassio and Roderigo as he is at presenting the darkness to Othello.

cast in his mood Cast off because of his (i.e. Othello's) bad temper.

speak parrot Say what I don't mean.

fustian Rubbish.

wherefore About it.

moraler Moralist.

Hydra A many-headed mythological monster. For every head cut off, two grew in its place.

unordinate Inordinate.

splinter Put a splint on.

And what's he . . . An example of Iago's black humour. His wickedness is stylishly self-conscious. His protestations of love and honesty are directed as much to the audience – with a wink – as to Cassio.

Probal to thinking Likely.

subdue Ask (successfully) for help.

fram'd as fruitful Made as generous.

her appetite i.e. Othello's appetite for Desdemona. Iago believes Othello will do anything she asks.

weak function Natural desire – to which he is vulnerable.

How am I then a villain . . . Note Iago's tone of mock-innocence. After all, he says, he really is doing what is best for Cassio – it just so happens that it forwards his own evil plan. Iago takes delight not only in doing evil and giving it the guise of good, but of it actually coming out of good.

Divinity of hell! i.e. I worship evil.
repeals Summons back.
wit Skill.
dilatory time Taking our time.
And thou ... Iago puts Cassio's downfall to Roderigo's credit.

Revision questions on Act II

1 What is the purpose of making the main characters arrive in Cyprus separately?
2 What qualities of Cassio's character are evident in this Act?
3 In what ways does the relationship between Iago and Othello develop?
4 How many different moods can you identify in this Act?
5 What is the significance of Act II in relation to the rest of the play?

Act III Scene 1

In an exchange full of the double entendres (double meanings, usually lewd) common in Shakespeare's low-life and comic scenes, Cassio persuades a clown (who has been sent down to dismiss musicians brought on by Cassio himself and who are disturbing Othello and Desdemona with their serenade) to tell Emilia that Cassio wishes to see her. Iago enters and agrees to fetch Emilia himself, which he then does. Emilia says that she will admit Cassio into Desdemona's presence.

Commentary

Iago's plan is going well: he has the satisfaction of appearing to help Cassio by offering to get Othello out of the way while the former lieutenant speaks to Desdemona, and he has manoeuvered both Cassio and Othello into the right situations for his own advantage. The first thirty lines of the scene take up the comic spirit of the previous scene, rather more lightheartedly, making the point – among others – that Cassio's problems are of little account to anyone but himself. His melancholy self-absorption and his eagerness to do the right thing mark him out as an easy victim for Iago, the successful working of whose plot depends on the contriving of a meeting between Cassio and Desdemona. That meeting is arranged in this scene.

tail Colloquial for – among other things – penis. This whole passage (lines 3–9) is a characteristic piece of bawdy in which the references are now so remote as to be obscure.

no more noise Othello does not like music. Moreover he must be weary of having his first hours with Desdemona disturbed.

keep up thy quillets Forget your quibbles.

shall seem to Arrange to.

In happy time What a fortunate meeting. Once again this is ironic: the meeting is fortunate for Iago because it allows him to set up his plan.

Florentine Cassio (from Florence) is inclined to mistrust Venetians. Ironically he trusts the least trustworthy Venetian.

displeasure Misfortune.

great affinity Well-connected.

safest occasion Best opportunity.

front Forelock.

Act III Scene 2

Othello gives Iago letters to deliver and then goes to visit the fortifications.

Commentary

The scene marks the passing of time and is characteristic of the way in which Shakespeare uses mosaic-patterns of long and short scenes – this one is just six lines – to vary the pace of his drama.

on the works On the fortifications.

Act III Scene 3

Desdemona agrees to speak to Othello on Cassio's behalf. As Cassio leaves, Othello and Iago enter, catching sight of him. Iago immediately starts to work on Othello's jealousy. With equal promptness Desdemona takes up Cassio's case, inflaming Othello's anger by her insistence that he should forgive Cassio. When Desdemona and Emilia leave, Iago returns to the attack, playing on Othello's impulsiveness and insinuating Desdemona's adultery with Cassio. The play's irony intensifies as Othello constantly refers to Iago's honesty even while Iago is most viciously and cruelly deceiving him – and, more disturbingly, as Othello's appetite for certainty about his wife's adultery grows:

he would rather believe her guilty than remain in doubt. This is Othello's low point in the play when his natural pride is transformed into a kind of abasement before Iago's evil dominance.

Iago shows his skill in the way he entices Othello to force him to speak, pretending that he would rather not. Once Othello's suspicions crystallize, Iago feels it is safe to advance possible reasons for Desdemona's adultery: the well-known unfaithfulness of Venetian women; her natural inconstancy, shown in the ease with which she left her father; the strangeness of her marriage with Othello. Iago is especially audacious in risking this last reason, for it touches Othello at his most sensitive point, his pride. The fact that Iago does dare to risk it suggests that Othello is altogether more vulnerable to the fact of being an outsider in Venice, a black man in a white man's world, than we had perhaps suspected. By accepting Iago's suggestion that Desdemona must be a strange girl to marry Othello in the first place, the general reaches the depths of pathos: the proud man whose pride is fuelled precisely by the sense of his own unworthiness.

When the general is left alone he broods on his deficiencies: being black, a rough soldier, exposed to the passions. At this point Emilia enters with Desdemona, who notices that Othello looks ill. He is indeed, but in soul, not body. The husband and wife leave, Desdemona accidentally dropping her handkerchief, which Emilia retrieves, commenting that Iago has often begged her to steal just this handkerchief for him. He then enters and takes the handkerchief from her. She leaves. In a brief soliloquy Iago announces his plan: he will incriminate Cassio by leaving the handkerchief in Cassio's lodging. At this point in the play, while Othello is at his low point, Iago is in the ascendant. Every chance seems to go his way — a fact which lulls him into a false sense of security in his own abilities.

Othello then returns, his suspicions at fever pitch. He wants absolute certainty, absolute proof of his wife's infidelity, threatening Iago with dire punishment if he doesn't make good his charges with evidence. For the first time Iago seems afraid: he has stirred the sleeping lion. He invents a story about Cassio talking in his sleep about love of Desdemona. Convinced now by the most unlikely tale, so desperate is he to be sure of his wife's guilt, Othello believes Iago. Appointing him lieutenant, Othello assigns to Iago Cassio's murder, declaring that he will undertake the death of Desdemona himself.

Commentary

This is the play's central scene. In it the die is irreversibly cast. Iago is now no longer even partly in control: Othello's passion sweeps them both on (see ll. 335–8, 'Look where he comes . . . owedst yesterday', where Iago recognizes this). We see what an altogether larger man than Iago Othello is, for all his weakness: uncalculating, absolute. On the other hand, central to the scene are the long discussions in which Iago manoeuvres Othello into position. Gradually Othello begins to adopt Iago's terminology, exchanging his terse, noble style of speech for incoherence and exclamations about animal lust. It is clear that while the plot hinges on trivial incidents, the real action is essentially psychological: what matters is not what people do but what others think they have done. The idea of deceit is crucial to the play for this reason – both of others and of the characters' selves. The play takes place, as it were, in their minds. What we see on stage is an outward image of this.

All my All in my.

honest Even Desdemona, like Cassio, echoes Othello's estimate of the Ensign.

Bounteous Desdemona is referred to throughout the play as bounteous and fruitful by Othello, Cassio, Roderigo and even Iago. The word suggests both generosity of character and endowment by nature with many gifts and virtues.

strangest Estrangement.

politic Judicious. Othello, she says, will favour Cassio as soon as it is sensible to do so. He must take account of the feelings of others.

nice and wat'rish Petty and thin.

breed . . . circumstance Get so that it fails to take up opportunities. Cassio doesn't want to leave things too long in case he is forgotten.

doubt Dread.

article Clause.

watch him tame Keep him awake until he does her will – a metaphor from training hawks.

his board a shrift His table a confessional.

solicitor Petitioner.

your discretion What you think best. Ironically, it is just Cassio's hasty retreat that inflames Othello's suspicions, primed by Iago.

Ha . . . Iago shows skill as an improvisor, exploiting the circumstances. His technique is always to imply a convincing explanation of things, without directly stating it.

reconciliation i.e. repentance.

an honest face . . . One of the play's many references to the contrast between open and deceitful natures. Desdemona is both right and wrong about herself: she judges Cassio rightly and Iago wrongly.

Why then, tomorrow ... Desdemona could hardly choose a more unfortunate moment to nag her husband.

in our common reason In the usual way of thinking.

not almost Hardly. Perhaps Desdemona forgets that Othello believes he has already treated Cassio leniently by not punishing him (see II. 3, 240).

mammering Hesitating.

in Back into favour.

boon Favour. Desdemona means that she is doing Cassio a favour which is really in Othello's best interest. Her enthusiasm for Cassio rubs salt into the wound.

poise Weight.

be it as your fancies teach you Behave in this foolish way if you like.

wretch Used here as a term of endearment, yet prefiguring Othello's treatment of her as an offender.

Chaos is come again Chaos will come. But chaos comes in spite of Othello's great love, and even because of it.

My noble lord ... From here (line 93) to line 283 Iago gradually induces Othello to believe in Desdemona's adultery. Then, from line 326 to line 486, they plan their monstrous campaign of proof and murder. You should notice the stages by which Iago corrupts Othello, so that the general even ends up using the same animal metaphors for sexuality that come so readily to Iago's tongue. First Iago offers vague hints, then refuses to say what he is hinting at: this secures Othello's obsessive curiosity. Then Iago begins to suggest more directly what he means ('Look to your wife; observe her well with Cassio.') He induces Othello to force him to reveal the exact nature of his suspicions, then finds reasons to base them on: the infidelity of Venetian women, Desdemona's deception of her father, the unnaturalness of her marriage with Othello. Knowing the tenacious quality of his master's passion, he is then able to let Othello brood. The poison will do its work: Othello will take the lead from Iago in discovering evidence, and all Iago need do is encourage him.

he echoes me ... He does indeed. By the end of the scene Iago and Othello are of one mind.

conceit Notion.

stops Hesitations.

close denotements i.e. they indicate something unspoken. Othello unconsciously points up his own blindness to Iago's true nature.

Men should be that they seem Iago is fond of this joke, which is made for his own benefit and that of the audience.

free to Free to decline.

leets and law-days Courts. Every man, Iago means, has impure thoughts at times.

his ear i.e. Othello's.

vicious Wrong.

As I . . . are not Iago seems to enjoy sailing near the wind. Here he describes what he is in fact doing i.e. inventing faults in others. 'Jealousy' means 'critical eye' here. This is a good description of Iago's own attitude to rumours of his wife's adultery. One of the many layers of irony involving Iago concerns his occasional tendency to tell the truth – in spite of himself.

Good name . . . souls Compare II, 3, 260, where Iago says exactly the opposite to Cassio.

Who dotes, yet doubts Iago here introduces a major motif of this scene: Othello's desperate need for certainty about Desdemona, one way or the other. Othello trusts where he should spurn and doubts where he should trust: brilliant in war, he shows lack of sense and judgement in private affairs. The disparity between the two is part of the tragedy in a play which focuses on the relationship between the public and the private.

fineless Without limit.

the changes of the moon Suspicions waxing and waning – a notion especially distressing to Othello, who prides himself on steadfastness and endurance of purpose.

exsufflicate and blown Inflated and swollen.

weak Slight.

franker . . . Iago has now inveigled Othello into demanding an explicit charge from him.

they i.e. wives.

their best conscience Their greatest care. In this speech Iago makes a direct charge against Desdemona, given full charter to do so by Othello's demand for certainty. To that extent Iago has judged his master's character well, accurately gauging the degrees of curiosity, jealousy, sexual pride and obsessiveness in Othello's nature. This is part of the tragedy because the general's very virtues turn against him: steadfastness becomes obstinacy; warmth becomes frenzy; protectiveness becomes possessiveness; love becomes anger.

close as oak Impermeable as oak-grain.

but I am much . . . Notice how Iago breaks off, as though he cannot bear to tell Othello the truth.

I see this hath a little Monumental understatement. Once again Iago is playing with his victim, enjoying the joke and the torment.

grosser issues Anything worse.

nor to larger reach i.e. this is only a suspicion, nothing more.

I see you are mov'd Iago continues to needle Othello: he knows that any rages must be directed now against Desdemona.

erring Wandering. Now Othello himself is finding reasons for believing in his wife's guilt.

Ay . . . repent Iago, picking up the word nature from Othello, develops a theme, outrageous, under the circumstances: for he tells Othello that it was extraordinary of a white girl to marry a black man in the first place, being an act against nature. She must, by this reckoning, be even more lecherous and untrustworthy than the normal run of Venetian women. 'Nature' here means what is fit, proper and normal.

affect Favour.

rank Overgrown.

fall Come.

country forms Fellow countrymen. The implication is that Desdemona may come to her senses and come to think of you as one of us. To suggest to Othello at this moment that his wife chose him precisely because of qualities which mark him out from her society is to make him feel even more insecure and an outsider, and therefore more passionate and hysterical.

set on Tell. Othello, who prides himself on frankness, stoops to spying.

This honest creature . . . unfolds Again ironic: Othello means more than he knows.

My lord . . . honour . . . Note how Iago returns, as if on impulse, to beg Othello to forget the whole business – knowing full well he can't – and then immediately suggests that he observe Desdemona more closely.

strain her entertainment Exaggerate her welcome. Othello and Iago are no longer master and man, but conspirators, with Iago taking the lead.

exceeding honesty Othello obsessively refers to Iago's honesty.

knows all qualities Ironic: Iago does indeed understand the baser passions but fatally misses the point of the higher ones.

haggard Wild.

jesses The straps fastening a hawk's legs to the leash. This takes up the hint of 'haggard', a word specifically applied to hawks.

at fortune At random.

soft parts Easy graces. The seed of self-doubt sown by Iago is at work.

chamberers Courtiers. The word has a hint of 'philanderers.'

keep a corner Not possess completely. This phrase indicates the absoluteness of Othello's character: he must be all or nothing.

Prerogativ'd . . . base Othello seems to mean that because the great are more in the public eye they are more vulnerable to shame and humiliation than the humble. That betrayal is common to all he says in the next line: 'Tis destiny.'

forked The cuckold or betrayed husband was traditionally pictured wearing horns – the visible sign of his humiliation.

I'll not believe it . . . Othello lurches from doubt to doubt.

forehead A pun: cuckold's horns are worn on top of the forehead.

wayward Inexplicable.

ta'en out Copied. One may wonder why Emilia does not speculate on Iago's repeated request for this handkerchief. Emilia's reference to his 'fantasy' is hardly satisfying: Iago is no more whimsical than he is interested in embroidery. This is a weak spot in Shakespeare's plotting, quickly covered over by the entry of Iago himself.

import Importance. Emilia regrets her actions. It may be that she has a faint notion that Iago means mischief.

Be not you known on't Never you mind.

conceits Fancies.

mines of sulphur Sulphur mines were supposed to burn perpetually, without being lit. There is also a hint here of Othello's hellish state.

mandragora A narcotic.

medicine Cure.

owedst Had.

He that is robb'd ... A pathetic echo of Iago's lines III, 3, 161–165. Robbery is a running theme throughout the play – sexual, material and moral.

Pioners Manual labourers.

the plumed troop ... Note how Othello instinctively links his love and his soldiering, continuing a link which runs through the play: if Desdemona proves false, nothing in his life can be good.

circumstance Ceremonial.

counterfeit Jove made thunder: the guns roar with the same sound.

prove ... Othello is now dangerous, like a wild animal: his wrath threatens to turn against even Iago.

Is't come to this? Ambiguous in meaning, but it may signify Iago's alarm at the tempest he has stirred up against himself.

probation Proof.

hinge, nor loop i.e. no visible joint or impediment.

amaz'd Horrified.

fool Iago is addressing himself. He affects a rough surliness, righteous indignation at Othello's aggressive behaviour. This is a new variation on his pose as the honest man.

By the world ... satisfied Othello is almost incoherent. Notice the way he jumps from phrase to phrase and idea to idea, especially in the contradictions of lines 387–96.

my name The idea of honour is important to Othello, as it was to Cassio (see II, 3, 254). Honour, in this view, is not merely a social matter: it is an attribute of the soul, for on it depends one's good name not only in life but after death.

Dian Diana, the goddess of chastity.

topp'd A pun: both beheaded and sexually possessed.

Death and damnation ... Othello rapidly loses all control of himself: his determination to kill Desdemona and Cassio is punctuated by hysterical outbursts.

bolster Share a pillow.

their own i.e. their own eyes.

prime Lecherous.

goats ... monkeys Othello later takes up these words (IV, 1, 259).

imputation Iago is admitting that he cannot show Othello his evidence: he can only recount it. Later he makes good this deficiency.

office Task.

sith Because.

loose of soul ... Othello will now swallow any nonsense, such as this story improvised by Iago. Once his mind is guided it will follow relentlessly, in spite of sense or reason.

be wise Iago can now take on the restraining role, while at the same time supplying further 'evidence.'

or any that was hers ... Note that Iago is now secure enough to supply Othello's words for him.

hearted In my heart.

aspics i.e. asps – small vipers.

Pontic Black.

Shall ne'er look back This confirms that one of Othello's virtues – his steadfastness – has become a positive vice: a mixture of obstinacy and credulity.

capable Thorough.

Do not rise yet ... The scene ends with a parody of marriage, in which Iago and Othello pledge themselves to one another: 'I am your own for ever,' says Iago (486), thus ensuring that Othello cannot retreat; giving the whole affair a momentousness beyond the mere desire for revenge. Even Iago's language – giving up hand and heart to obey Othello – echoes the marriage service.

lights Stars.

clip Surround.

excellency Power.

remorse Pity. Iago means that his obedience to Othello's will, whatever he shall command, will show his pity for the general.

My friend Cassio. Not only is this ironic – Iago is Cassio's worst enemy – but it also gives Iago the lever he needs (*My* friend ... *yours*) to ask for Desdemona's reprieve, knowing it will not be granted.

fair devil The phrase expresses exactly the conflict in Othello's mind between love and hatred. It echoes Iago's 'Divinity of hell'.

Act III Scene 4

Desdemona and Emilia enter in search of Cassio. Desdemona questions Emilia about the whereabouts of the handkerchief. Othello then comes on stage, distracted. When Desdemona – perhaps insensitively – tells him she has sent for Cassio, he replies by asking obsessively for the handkerchief, storming out when he is told she doesn't have it. Iago and Cassio then enter to plead Cassio's suit. They discuss Othello's strange behaviour with Desdemona and Emilia, who then leave. Cassio's mistress Bianca comes in and Cassio asks her to copy the handkerchief he has found in his room.

Commentary

After the psychological and emotional intensity of the previous scene this part of the play moves with relative speed. It is clearly evident here how Shakespeare prefers to concentrate the audience's attention on motivation and inward development, the physical action being subordinated to these. The almost ridiculous coincidence that Desdemona, Othello and Cassio should all ask after the handkerchief demonstrates not only its symbolic role in the drama but also Shakespeare's relative lack of interest in plot realism. The point of this scene is to focus all our attention on the handkerchief so that we shall be well aware of its significance in what follows. By abruptly juxtaposing the different responses of the three characters – Othello, Desdemona and Cassio – Shakespeare makes the likely outcome glaringly obvious. Far from detracting from the suspense, this intensifies it, focusing all our concentration on what we know now to be the almost inevitable outcome: Othello's discovery of the handkerchief and his subsequent murderous rage. To emphasize a point made before: the triviality of the object only intensifies the enormity of the crime – based on such flimsy evidence – and the pathos of the contrast between cause and result.

lies i.e. lodges.
stabbing To risk being stabbed. The rather weak pun on 'lies' (lodges/deceives) is characteristic of Shakespeare's word-play. In this context, however, the clown's playfulness contrasts favourably with Iago's malign deceitfulness.
catechize Question.
by them answer i.e. by means of the answers to my questions I will answer *your* question.
moved Interceded with.
compass Range.
Where should I lose ... Desdemona's mind runs anxiously on the handkerchief. Her next speech shows she has a glimmering of what may happen. Emilia tells a lie, and the perils of lying (described a few lines earlier by the clown), are to be visited on her with a vengeance in the play's last scene.
crusadoes Portuguese gold coins.
my noble Moor ... Alone among the characters in the play Desdemona remains constant to the end.
ill Suspicious.
humours Temperamental inclinations. Desdemona's ignorance of

Othello's state is both moving and alarming. Her innocence proves to be her downfall.

this hand is moist Moistness of the palm is supposed to be a sign of sexual desire.

liberal Othello means *over*-liberal. Fruitful and liberal both have the double connotation of 'generous' and 'promiscuous'.

sequester Seclusion.

sweating devil Lust. Othello cannot refrain from accusing his wife.

I cannot speak of this I don't know what you mean.

chuck Dear.

sullen rheum Runny nose, cold. Othello tries to hide his fury at the mention of Cassio's name.

Lend me thy handkerchief Once again Shakespeare ignores probability in the interest of dramatic effect and concentration.

Egyptian Gypsy. Whether true or not, Othello's story is clearly meant as an unmistakable hint to Desdemona: the handkerchief stands for faithfulness and sexual purity.

charmer i.e. maker of charms.

A sybil . . . compasses A two hundred year old prophetess.

mummy Juice of embalmed dead bodies.

maidens' hearts . . . Othello harps on the theme of purity.

startingly In fits and starts. Othello's passion is now unavoidably obvious to Desdemona. He is looking for confirmation of his suspicions.

Is't lost? i.e. the handkerchief.

Cassio . . . While Othello hysterically asks again and again about the handkerchief, Desdemona repeats her request about Cassio. She thinks to calm him with this, but for Othello it must be further proof of her guilt: that the man's name is the first thing which comes to mind when he taxes her with loss of handkerchief.

Is not this man jealous? Emilia's reiteration of her question after this violent interchange needs no answer.

'Tis not a year . . . Emilia attempts to divert the conversation into her usual common-sense channel – uneasy about her role in removing the handkerchief.

the happiness All will be well.

But . . . benefit Just. It seems that Cassio, like Othello, prefers certainty to doubt.

So shall . . . content I'll make the best of a bad job.

shut myself up in Work out.

alms Favour.

advocation Pleading.

My lord is not my lord . . . Compare Iago's 'I am not what I am' (I, 1, 65). This is one of the references in the play to people being true or not to their natures – references which bring into question what those natures are. Is Othello's 'true' self the noble, generous soldier, or the raving, savage Moor?

favour Appearance.

humour Disposition.

blank Bull's-eye, line of fire.

unhatch'd practice Undiscovered plot.

puddled Clouded.

inferior things . . . Desdemona is psychologically accurate when she says a great trouble may make men snappish over minor matters, but she mistakes the nature of Othello's cause for grief.

indues Leads to.

members Limbs.

Men are not gods This proves to be painfully true of Othello.

unhandsome warrior Inadequate soldier. The phrase means that her fears and doubts have made Desdemona fall below her proper confidence and trust in Othello – especially as she is a general's wife (for which see II, 1, 182). We must not perpetually be expecting from a man the attentions of a new-married 'bridal'.

Arraigning Accusing.

suborn'd bribed.

the witness i.e. the doubts and fears of her soul.

cause A word later echoed by Othello just before he murders his wife (see V, 2, 1).

monster The word Iago also uses. In view of what the audience know Desdemona's hope is ironic.

Eight score eight Eight score plus eight. Observe the light flirtatious tone of Bianca reproaching Cassio for his neglect, and compare it with the exchanges earlier in the scene between Othello and his wife.

dial Clock.

Pardon me Cassio's reply is pompous and distant in tone, at first.

Strike off this score of Make up to you for this.

felt absence Absence I have felt. Bianca's reproaches are a parody of Othello's frenzy.

Go to Come on.

demanded Asked for. Cassio, like Emilia, wants the fatal handkerchief copied.

addition Credit. It seems Cassio himself is not, after all, above deceiving Othello.

woman'd In the company of a woman. Cassio is somewhat hypocritical and priggish: he wants to get on by pandering to what he believes are the General's prejudices.

you do not love me Echoing his words, Bianca shows herself more of a realist.

circumstanc'd Satisfied with things as they are.

Revision questions on Act III

1 Give a detailed account of what happens in Scene 3.
2 What is Emilia's significance in this Act?
3 What characteristic imagery does Iago use?
4 In what ways does violence figure in this Act?
5 What aspects does Shakespeare present of the relationship between public business and private life?

Act IV Scene 1

Iago pretends to 'defend' Desdemona before Othello as he defended Cassio, in order to incriminate her more thoroughly. He can now well afford to do this. So distressed is Othello that he falls into a trance: the noble calmness and rationality of his early scenes are dissipated, their place taken by blind, conflicting passions. It is the conflict of these passions – pride and self-hatred, love and loathing – which fatally weakens Othello and leads him to acquiesce in Iago's darkest hints.

While Othello lies dazed on the ground, Cassio comes in briefly and Iago arranges to speak to him later. When Othello recovers, Iago suggests that the general watch his talk with Cassio, which he does, assuming that they are discussing Desdemona. The exchanges are really about Cassio's mistress Bianca, who is the cause of the coarse remarks and laughter. Bianca then opportunely comes on stage with Desdemona's handkerchief – another apparently fortunate coincidence for Iago, seeming to confirm his story of the handkerchief's whereabouts. When Cassio leaves we see Othello torn between grief and murderous rage. Iago gruesomely advises him to strangle Desdemona in their marriage bed, as a fitting punishment for adultery, and Othello agrees to do so. It is arranged that Iago will murder Cassio himself – repeating what had been decided in a previous scene.

At this point Desdemona enters, accompanied by a messenger from Venice, who announces Othello's recall from Cyprus and Cassio's appointment in his place. When Desdemona expresses her pleasure at Cassio's promotion Othello loses his self-control and strikes her, to the astonishment of the messenger.

Commentary

The stratagems (such as spying) to which Othello stoops in this scene are clear proof of the moral depths to which he has sunk. Iago is now completely dominant, as shown by his casual treatment of Othello as he swoons on the floor. The arrival of the messenger reminds us of a Venice we might have forgotten by now, such is the isolated intensity of the action in Cyprus in this scene and the previous one. The outside world, so apparent in the early scenes of the play, vanishes for a while as the drama is played out among a handful of characters: Othello, Iago, Desdemona, Cassio. There is a claustrophobic quality in this scene, emphasized by the spying and Othello's hysteria.

Will you think so?... Like the play's opening scene, Act IV Scene 1 begins in the middle of a conversation, but this time Iago's dupe is Othello. The parallelism between the General and Roderigo, who began so far apart, emphasizes to what similar positions they have come: pathetically dependent on the patronage of Iago. What strikes the reader is the reversal of roles since the previous Act: now Othello is making statements and Iago asks the questions – exactly the outcome he wanted.

Naked abed... Iago's suggestions have become almost ludicrous in their outrageousness, pretending to suggest that kissing and sleeping naked with another man might just be innocent. His pleasure at playing with the gullible Othello is evident throughout the exchanges.

hypocrisy against the devil i.e. pretending to be sinful, so as to cheat the devil.

do so i.e. sleep naked with another man.

venial Trivial.

handkerchief Iago knows how to arouse Othello's temper by mentioning this.

Her honour . . . not Compare II, 3, 254.

raven A sign of ill-omen: also supposed to be a spreader of sickness.

had my handkerchief... The handkerchief has now become a way of referring to Desdemona herself.

What if ... Iago always begins with suggestion.

him There is now no need to name Cassio.

knaves be such abroad There are such fools about.

dotage of some mistress Devotion of a mistress.

supplied them Gratified their desire. The sense of this involved passage is simply: some men, having gratified their desire by constant pursuit of a woman, or because a woman is attracted to them, are silly enough to gossip about it. Iago implies that Cassio is one such.

I know not what... Iago is still playing with Othello. By lengthening the torture he will intensify it.

Lie . . . Iago's prevarication here echoes the clown in III, 4, 1–18. With 'belie' Othello frantically takes up the wordplay in a very different manner.

Lie with her, lie on her . . . Othello reaches a pitch of incoherent frenzy in this speech, as Iago comes out with his damning equivocation on 'lie' – leaving Othello to state the conclusion. The General finally collapses, so overcome is he by this explicit revelation of the 'truth'.

shadowing passion These words seems to refer to whatever is darkening Othello's mind, i.e. his jealousy.

some instruction Good reason. In his distraction Othello now takes his own desperate state as 'evidence' that there must be something wrong about Desdemona. Othello's weaknesses become the evidence for Desdemona's supposed weaknesses.

it is not words . . . Iago has brought vividly before Othello the actuality of Desdemona's adultery by means of the handkerchief. On another level we might take the words to mean that it is physical passion, not mere words, which so affects Othello – that is the hint of 'noses, ears, lips'.

lethargy i.e. fit.

straight Soon. There is a sort of comedy about the way in which the characters come and go from the stage at just the right moments, as though Iago were controlling them – symbolic, perhaps, of the sense in which he *does* direct their fates.

Dost thou mock me? This refers directly to Iago's question 'have you not hurt your head?' – but according to the way the actor says it, we might take the line as hinting either at Othello's sense of how low he has sunk, or his faint momentary suspicion that Iago's story is just too good (i.e. bad) to be true.

like a man Perhaps Iago's cruellest piece of patronage to the otherwise brave and virile Othello. To Iago a man is one who cultivates his interests at the expense of others, and who debases reason, man's noblest gift, to the service of low desires.

A horned man A cuckold.

monster . . . This idea recurs (see III, 4, 159). As an outsider and a black man, Othello has always been something of a monster in Venetian society: now he is becoming one to himself. This is the theme of questionable identity surfacing again. 'Civil' refers to life in the city.

yok'd Married. Ironic.

draw i.e. bear the burden of marriage.

unproper i.e. not their own.

they dare swear peculiar They confidently believe to be theirs alone.

your case is better . . . Iago, taking up Othello's own view, says it is preferable to be certain of the worst than to live in ignorance. Such is the intensifying irony of the situation that by now almost everything Iago says is either the opposite of the truth or a misapplication of it.

lip Kiss.

No, let me . . . shall be Knowing my own roving eye – and that of other men – I can guess at the behaviour of women.

Confine . . . list Be patient. Shakespeare is not always more condensed in expression than modern speech, as this phrase shows.

erewhile Earlier.

unsuiting such a man . . . Iago here plays on Othello's sense of his own dignity. He can say what he likes to the general now.

ecstasy i.e. distraction.

encave Hide.

cope Have sexual relations with.

all in spleen Temperamental, unpredictable.

housewife Here the word means something like 'slut'.

as 'tis . . . one The prostitute is desired by many men, but herself desires only one.

unbookish Uninformed. Othello will draw false conclusions because he doesn't know the truth.

conster Construe.

addition Title, i.e. of Lieutenant.

kills me . . . The excessive terms Cassio habitually uses to remark on his disfavour suggest a tendency to self-pity and dramatization. Cassio is certainly not an heroic or even very admirable character.

Ply . . . well Keep on pressing your case.

caitiff Wretch.

faintly Without conviction.

customer Prostitute.

bear . . . wit Think better of my judgment.

scor'd me Taken advantage of me.

flattery i.e. she flatters herself.

bauble Trollop. Cassio's cynical treatment of Bianca, while entirely lacking Iago's ruthlessness, is discernibly related to his contempt for women.

fitchew Polecat – noted for its strong scent and lustfulness.

dam Wife. How opportune for Iago's plot is the entrance of Bianca, babbling of the handkerchief.

take out i.e. copy.

piece of work Both 'needlework' and 'story'. Bianca has been brooding, like Othello, on the unfaithfulness of her lover, and has returned to reproach him. Once again the minor parts reflect the major ones.

hobby-horse Prostitute.

I would . . . sweet woman Othello see-saws from one idea to another, from Cassio to Desdemona.

a-killing Being killed. In his highly-wrought state Othello is easily fooled.

And let her rot . . . tasks Again Othello see-saws: here he passes directly from one sentiment jealous hatred – to its opposite – idealisation of Desdemona.

Nay ... Iago is disconcerted by Othello's sudden revolt in favour of Desdemona.

gentle Well-bred.

the pity of it This repeated phrase goes to the heart – the more so because of its violent context.

patent Full permission.

unprovide my mind Weaken my resolution.

atone i.e. bring them together.

Fire and brimstone! ... There are two conversations going on here: (1) between Lodovico and Desdemona, and (2) between Desdemona and Othello. Both men misconstrue the situation and the conversations collide violently when Othello strikes his wife.

crocodile The reference is to crocodile i.e. false, tears.

Ay, you did wish ... avaunt ... Othello intermittently loses and regains control of herself. Now everything, however tenuous the connection, has become part of his obsession – even Lodovico's request for Desdemona to be called back.

Goats and monkeys ... Animal images pervade the play, hinting at the bestial nature of human beings. See also III, 3, 409.

He is much chang'd ... Again the identity theme appears. Lodovico's arrival is an apt moment for making the point that Othello is not the man he was – a point made by Iago in crueller fashion (IV, 1, 77). earlier in the play.

He's that he is ... he were ... This contrasts ironically with the words of Iago which it echoes from I, 1, 65.

if, as he might, he is not If he is not what he might be. From here to the end of the scene Iago uses his favourite technique of innuendo, seeming to defend Othello, but damning him.

his own courses will denote him ... This is supremely ironic, for it echoes what Othello has said throughout the play, namely that he is what he seems. Iago now turns this argument against him.

I am deceiv'd ... The line piles irony on irony. That Lodovico should say this of the victim Othello to the arch-deceiver Iago ...

Act IV Scene 2

Under Othello's close questioning Emilia vigorously defends her mistress. She fetches Desdemona and leaves her with Othello, who abuses his wife without specifying his charges of adultery beyond calling her a whore in general. He leaves Desdemona upset and confused. Emilia then brings in Iago, who advises Desdemona to shrug off the matter as one of Othello's tantrums. As in his treatment of the General, Iago clearly derives pleasure from patronizing the worried Desdemona.

Ironically, Emilia is acute enough to perceive that someone

has poisoned Othello's mind, without being able to work out who it is. The scene ends with another exchange between Iago and Roderigo, who is annoyed with the Ensign for not delivering Desdemona to him as promised and paid for. Iago casually diverts Roderigo's anger against Cassio, with some success, though Roderigo is no longer quite so easily satisfied as hitherto.

Commentary

This scene makes it clear that Iago's treatment of Roderigo runs parallel to his dealings with Othello. Both are taken in by the Ensign, and both are fooled as to Desdemona's nature. Roderigo thus serves as a foil to Othello, but also points up the differences between them. Roderigo is a trivial fool, a rich, idle trifler whose fate is pathetic. Othello is a serious character, a man of substance and achievement whose downfall is truly tragic because it is large and lofty enough, and because he falls from such a height. Roderigo, meanwhile, remains his silly self, whether filled with hope or with despair.

You have seen nothing ... Again the scene opens on an urgent, conversational note. The play moves with great speed in the last two acts, after the monumental crisis of Act III, Scene 3.

nor ever did suspect ... Emilia is telling the truth. On the other hand, she is compromised by her behaviour in the matter of the handkerchief.

If any wretch ... The first of Emilia's blind guesses at the truth.

serpent's curse God's curse on the serpent.

simple bawd Mere procuress.

cannot Dare not.

this is a subtle whore i.e. Desdemona.

And yet she'll kneel ... Othello accuses his wife of hypocrisy and deceit. In his very next line he addresses this 'whore' as 'dear'. Such is the power of self-deception, he does not notice his own hypocrisy.

chuck See note on III, 4, 45.

Some of your function Do what you usually do, guard the door (as in a brothel).

procreants Lovers. In the circumstances, dishonest and ironic.

mystery Business.

import Mean. For all her dread, Desdemona cannot credit the idea of Othello's suspicions.

Swear thou art honest ... The word 'honest' takes on a protean quality within the play. Desdemona is honest because she is the opposite of the 'honest Iago' – another example of values being turned on their heads.

my father . . . This is the nearest she can get to understanding Othello's rage.

Had it pleas'd Heaven . . . There is more than a tinge of self-pity in this speech. Othello is quite taken up with his own feelings and dignity.

A fixed figure . . . This echoes the point made several times in the play about loss of reputation. 'Fixed' because once a man is betrayed and known to be so, that name stays with him always.

garner'd up my heart Concentrated all my love.

Knot and gender Copulate.

Turn thy complexion there Change colour, indeed. No doubt, Desdemona has gone pale.

shambles Slaughterhouse.

quicken even with blowing Come to life as soon as the eggs are laid. The sense is obscure. Responding to the word 'honest' as meaning chaste, Othello is perhaps comparing Desdemona to the flies in the casualness and speed of their breeding and birth: so is she sexually profligate with her favours. Notice how he reaches for animal images now, as Iago does, when he speaks of sex.

What committed? Othello again takes a word in another sense. Desdemona speaks of committing an offence: for her husband the word is linked with the committing of adultery. Misunderstanding (of the sort seen in IV, 1, 225–78) is a constant feature of the relations between Othello and his wife. Part of their tragedy is a failure of communication. Whatever Othello may say about words (e.g. IV, 1, 41) much turns on them.

commoner Prostitute.

Heaven stops . . . hear't As in II, 1, 68–87, Desdemona is made the object of the elements' attention – but now it is their disgust, not their rapture she is said to inspire.

Saint Peter The keeper of Heaven's gate.

your pains Your efforts. Othello addresses Emilia as though she were a bawd.

half asleep . . . Just as Othello earlier fell into a swoon, so now Desdemona is in a trance of misery.

water Tears. Since she cannot weep she cannot answer.

our wedding sheets . . . Desdemona seems to have the same idea as Iago: that her marriage-bed will be the scene of final catastrophe.

'Tis meet It is right. Ironic: Desdemona knows she has done nothing wrong.

opinion i.e. censure.

so bewhor'd her Called her whore. Emilia has been eavesdropping.

heavy terms Insults.

callat Slut.

I do not know . . . Because she speaks nothing but the truth, Desdemona does not have the torrent of words at Iago's command.

eternal Meddling.

busy and insinuating rogue A good enough description of Iago, which draws irony from being addressed to him. He dismisses the suggestion.

cogging, cozening Cheating (the words are synonyms). Emilia strongly suspects much of the truth about Iago in this scene.

halter Rope.

Speak within doors Speak quietly. Iago is unnerved by Emilia's grasp of the situation. He may fear that with her knowledge about the handkerchief she can piece together the facts.

seamy side Suspicious side. Emilia moves further towards the truth, as Iago's irritable reply indicates.

in any other form With anyone else.

abhor me Disgust me. Desdemona has now found her tongue. Oblivious to the discussion between Emilia and Iago she concentrates single-mindedly on the statement of her innocence and her revulsion at adultery.

addition Name. Desdemona's humility and love contrast markedly with Othello's hurt pride and possessive jealousy.

How now, Roderigo? . . . The last in the series of lengthy conversations between Roderigo and Iago. While there is no true sub-plot in the play, Iago's trickery of Roderigo comes near to one, and the parallel of Roderigo and Othello is made more explicit as the play progresses — here by divergence: where Othello trusts Iago unreservedly, the silly Roderigo has his doubts and gives voice to them. This is ironic: though a fool, Roderigo seems to have more sense than Othello in detecting the unsatisfactory parts of Iago's behaviour.

doffest Put off.

all conveniency Everything I need.

votarist Nun. In this speech Roderigo makes very explicit the relationship he has with Iago: this is the mysterious deal they are discussing in the first scene of the play.

I cannot go to, man Notice the petulant, peevish tone of Roderigo here – a perfect index of his foolishness.

fopp'd Fooled.

You have said now That's more like it. Iago pretends to admire Roderigo's more resolute approach.

intendment Intention.

most just exception Serious misunderstanding.

wit and judgement Insight and justice. Iago half implies he accepts the intended rebuke and half that he has been testing Roderigo.

devise engines for Contrive schemes against.

compass Possibility.

linger'd Prolonged.

determinate Conclusive.

you shall be satisfied . . . These words take on a sinister meaning in retrospect when Iago kills Roderigo shortly afterwards.

Act IV Scene 3

After a supper in honour of Lodovico, the messenger from Venice, Othello sends Desdemona to bed. She is apprehensive and talks to her maid Emilia about women unfortunate in love, singing a melancholy old song on the subject. Emilia replies with sturdy commonsense comments on the weaknesses of the male sex. Desdemona then sends her away, as instructed by Othello.

Commentary

The trustingness and loyalty of Desdemona's character, despite her doubts and fears, are apparent in this exquisite lyrical scene, heightened by the coarse comments of Emilia, who manages to be right and wrong at the same time – right about how most people live but wrong about Desdemona's destiny, which, like Othello's, is loftier and more dreadful than the common run. The use of music in this scene makes so much clear, emphasizing the ethereal quality of Desdemona's character. Like Ophelia in *Hamlet* she goes singing to her death. Shakespeare often associates the intense, pure, passionate sexuality of young women with music in this way, their music being at once sensuous and yet not gross – unlike the drinking songs in Act II Scene 3. But there is another level to Shakespeare's use of music, for he commonly associates it with moments of great wonder or mystery, such as Desdemona's premonition of her death, which we have here.

The scene gives us a moment of lyrical quiet before the final storm of murder and suicide, made the more painful by our expectation of what is to come. It is also appropriate that Desdemona and Emilia should discuss the theme that has run right through the play: the question of relationships between man and woman. In this respect Emilia's commonsense is as ironic as Desdemona's song is pathetic: the weak jealousy of men that she describes is to be horrifically demonstrated before the night is out.

incontinent i.e. immediately.
Dismiss me? Emilia's question seems filled with foreboding.
All's one It's all the same. Desdemona rebukes the fancy she had for putting her wedding sheets on the bed. Yet in the very next line she speaks of her own death. Unsettled, she is becoming contradictory,

like her husband, in all but the constancy of her love for him.

talk i.e. to no purpose.

My mother . . . forsake her . . . As with Othello's story of the handkerchief (III, 4, 53–66) there is an obvious analogy here with Desdemona's own situation.

I have much to do It is as much as I can do not to.

proper Well-made.

nether Lower. Emilia's hyperbole contrasts with the commonsense remarks she makes about men later in the scene, but it takes up the notion expressed in Desdemona's story of Barbary about women distracted by love.

Sing willow . . . The willow was symbolic of unhappy love, appearing in the choruses of many melancholy 16th-century songs. The quiet and darkness of the night, the isolation of the bedroom, the premonitions of the two women, all make the scene intensely dramatic. By singing Desdemona emphasizes her gentle, delicate, even fragile qualities, and her femininity. This is the *lyrical* climax of the play: the *dramatic* climax occurs in the last scene.

I call'd . . . moe men The relevance of these words to Desdemona's situation is clear: the speaker in the song is a man, whose attitude contrasts with Othello's.

moe More.

'Tis neither here . . . Emilia tries to calm her mistress.

women do abuse . . . Desdemona takes up the theme of the song.

I might do it . . . Notice the counterpoint between Emilia's 'realistic' attitude and Desdemona's passionate idealism.

joint-ring Ring made in two halves.

lawn Linen.

Why, the wrong . . . right . . . Emilia's words have an uncomfortable touch of Iago's cynicism here – the line between sense and cynicism is a thin one.

to the vantage In addition.

store i.e. populate.

And pour . . . laps There is a double entendre here. By extension 'lap' can mean 'thigh': the reference is to sexual intercourse; 'they make love to other women'.

scant . . . despite Cut our allowance to spite us.

galls Tantrums.

sense . . . There is a hint here of the sexual pleasure to be obtained through the senses.

sport Lechery.

affection Passion.

ills i.e. bad deeds.

Not to . . . mend Not to follow bad examples but to learn from them. Desdemona replies with a sententious couplet to Emilia's claim for women's equality of rights in love with men. Emilia argues that women have desires and feelings as men do – a fact men too often forget.

Furthermore, if we behave badly, she says, we learn the example from men: 'their ills instruct us so'. This is an indirect indictment of Othello who can only suspect his wife because he is capable of imagining – or has experienced – things outside her knowledge.

Revision questions on Act IV

1 List the coincidences in this Act. Are there too many for credibility? What is their effect?
2 What is the effect of Act IV Scene 3, and how is it achieved?
3 In what ways does dramatic irony operate in this Act and why?
4 To what extent would you say that Iago is carried along by events in this Act, and to what extent does he control them?
5 Indicate the part played by Bianca in this Act.

Act V Scene 1

Iago has persuaded Roderigo to attack Cassio, which he now does. Roderigo comes off worst from the encounter, however. Hearing the row, Othello assumes that Iago has killed Cassio in the dark; he goes off to murder Desdemona, horribly inspired by this example. Iago enters and takes the opportunity to finish off Roderigo, thus removing the witness and accomplice to his plots. He then tries to implicate Bianca in the attack and sends Emilia off to find Othello — knowing, presumably, that she is likely to find him in the act of murder or bending over Desdemona's corpse.

Commentary

Once physical action replaces psychological and emotional development, things happen very quickly. Shakespeare is typical of the Jacobean dramatists in his ability to suggest chaos and violence with great economy. He also adds a twist to the plot by making Iago's plan appear to work. The darkness in which the scene takes place reminds us of the darkness in which the play began, and is clearly symbolic of the murky regions of the heart in which Iago hatches his plots, also of the confusion in which he has involved the other characters. As in *Macbeth* and *Hamlet*, Shakespeare uses darkness to great dramatic effect, entirely

through suggestion. It is all there in the words. Thus Othello's
<u>mistake – thinking Iago has killed Cassio – becomes sympto-
matic of his mistakes, factual and moral, throughout the play.</u>

bulk Shop-front.
put it home i.e. use it to kill.
It makes us . . . us Success or failure depends on it.
I have . . . he dies . . . The almost hypnotic power of Iago's persuasion
  is made clear by this testimony.
quat Pimple.
to the sense To the quick. Iago means that he has aroused Roderigo's
  passions to such a pitch that he will do almost anything.
He calls . . . large He will demand from me the gold and jewels he gave
  me.
bobb'd from Screwed out of. Slang.
It must not be This is the moment when Iago decides on Roderigo's
  death.
daily beauty One of many hints that Iago is specifically jealous of men
  more sexually attractive than he is.
unfold me Reveal my stratagem.
The voice of Cassio Another of Othello's fatal misunderstandings: he
  deduces from Cassio's cries that Iago is in the process of killing him.
minion Favourite – in a disparaging sense.
hies Advances.
Forth of Out of.
Thy bed . . . Othello, Iago and Desdemona are all preoccupied with the
  marriage-bed as the scene of reckoning.
no passage? i.e. is that a passer-by?
heavy Dark.
into the cry Where the cry comes from.
spoil'd Seriously hurt.
O murderous slave . . . Iago takes the opportunity to put one witness to
  his crimes out of the way. The darkness gives him cover.
As you shall prove us . . . Lodovico means: Ask, and you'll find out.
  'Prove' means 'to have experience of', and 'praise' something like
  'estimate', 'appraise'.
look you pale? . . . Of course she does, in the face of such carnage, and
  her lover injured, but Iago seizes on the fact and proceeds to
  improvise by hinting at Bianca's guilt.
whoring Iago returns to his favourite theme, implying that the quarrel
  has been about Bianca.
do you shake . . . Again the question is addressed to Bianca. The only
  one not surprised by the incident, Iago is confident enough to take
  control of the situation.
dress'd i.e. his wounds.
Emilia, run you . . . Iago wants the murder of Desdemona to be

discovered by someone else. He may calculate that Othello is far too
proud to implicate his loyal Lieutenant in the deed. On the other hand
Cassio is still alive; it would help if the others would leave, giving Iago
the chance to finish Cassio off.

makes me i.e. successful.

fordoes me Ruins me.

Act V Scene 2

Othello stands by his wife's bed as she sleeps, meditating in
torment on the deed he is about to commit. When she wakes he
refuses her pleas for mercy and strangles her. Stunned with
shock and grief, he unlocks the door to admit Emilia, who has
been shouting outside. She comes in to discover the dying Desdemona and to reproach Othello with her murder. Although
Desdemona's last words absolve him, Othello confesses, having
at first nervously denied his guilt. He tells Emilia that it was Iago
who enlightened him about Desdemona's adultery, and Emilia
realizes that her suspicion in Act IV scene 2 was justified: she
now knows who poisoned Othello's mind. Iago arrives. When
Emilia accuses him of treachery, refusing to be silent, he tries to
stab her, but is restrained by the people crowding into the room
after him. Succeeding a moment later in killing his wife after she
has proclaimed his guilt, he manages to escape but is caught and
brought back. He refuses to speak, though wounded by Othello.
After a confession of his own crime and a threnody over Desdemona's body, Othello kills himself.

Commentary

Central to this scene are Othello's magnificent speeches, which
vividly chart the final rapid progress of his mind. In the first
speech (lines 1–22) he is torn between determination to kill
Desdemona and awe at the thought of the deed's irreversibility;
in the second, when he has just committed the murder (92–102),
the repetitions and broken syntax show Othello distracted with
grief. The third (260–83) expresses his tragic recognition that
no man can control his fate, however powerful. The fourth
speech (339–57) is a return to the heroic lyricism of Othello's
earliest speeches in the play, in which he offers a comment on
his own past achievements, now purged of pride, and leading to
one of the play's most dramatic strokes: his suicide. His final

speech shows us Othello regaining his self-possession, and Othello tragically destroyed.

The play's final irony is that Iago achieves his desire – the downfall of Othello and Desdemona – even at the cost of his own, indicated in Lodovico's last speech which takes up many strands of the drama's imagery: poisoning; hell; animals; the marriage-bed; the sea.

It is the cause ... What the cause is remains uncertain: judging from the mention of 'chaste stars' in line 2, we must assume Othello refers to Desdemona's supposed adultery. This soliloquy brings out the divided nature of Othello's mind. 'I'll not shed her blood', he says at one moment, and then 'she must die' a few seconds later.

whiter skin He lingers over Desdemona's physical beauty.

more men ... This is a reason devised by Othello's jealous frenzy, not by the sense of justice he claims.

and then put out the light ... Note the repetitions in this speech, which heighten its intensity. Likewise the contrast between whiteness/stars/light and darkness/blood/death – a contrast which reflects the division in Othello's mind.

once put out thine ... The candle can be lit again but Desdemona's life, once extinguished, will be gone for ever. Othello is overawed by the irreversibility of his proposed act.

Promethean In Greek mythology, Prometheus was the half-god/half-man who brought fire down from heaven to men.

relume Rekindle.

this sorrow's heavenly This is an oxymoron, i.e. a pair of terms that seem to contradict each other; and the speech culminates in it and the following line, which also joins together two opposite ideas. In fact the whole soliloquy is a series of apparent oppositions. The syntax of the speech is also remarkable: it falls into a series of clauses connected not so much by logic as by association, twisting and turning between the two opposite impulses – love and hate – in Othello's mind, finally resolved into the synthesis of the last two lines.

Solicit Beg pardon.

forfend Forbid.

sins/They are loves ... i.e. Desdemona's only excesses are in love for Othello.

kills for loving Desdemona here reverses Othello's thought in line 22.

conceit Assurance.

warranty Permission. Desdemona means that she liked Cassio as a friend.

perjur'd woman Twice Othello accuses her of perjury.

murder ... sacrifice ... Othello's distinction is chilling. He can justify Desdemona's death as a sacrifice to justice: he is not so sure about killing her for personal motives.

ta'en order for it Made sure of it.

My great revenge Othello's hyperbole smacks of self-justification.

betray'd ... undone Othello takes these words as a confirmation of his suspicions. In his obsession everything contributes to the conclusion he has already reached.

My lord, my lord! Emilia takes up Desdemona's cry with another meaning, referring to Othello. The verbal echo is typical of Shakespeare's fondness for word-play at the most critical moments of his work.

she's dead ... Othello's speech is broken, distracted.

The noise was here Presumably Desdemona's cries and pleas: now she has the silence of death. In the immediate aftermath of his violence Othello is shocked.

she stirs ... she come ... The confusion of Emilia and Desdemona is the confusion of Othello's mind.

My wife The repetitions mark the misery of Othello's realization.

eclipse ... yawn An allusion to the traditional association between earthly and heavenly catastrophes.

What, now? ... Othello is quite distracted: he has forgotten about Cassio and Iago.

error The movements of the moon (Luna) controlled the state of lunatics, according to the 16th-century view: the nearer she came to earth, the worse they got.

falsely murder'd i.e. murdered for something she did not do. Desdemona's revival is only just made acceptable by dramatic effect: it borders on the ludicrous.

You heard her say The full depths of Othello's debasement are revealed in this line: the haughty general trembles at the enormity of his own deed – not, we may suppose, from fear of the judicial consequences but from shame, confusion and humiliation.

She's like a liar ... From here to line 136 Emilia and Othello exchange a strange litany of opposites: lies and truth; fire and water; angel and devil.

false as water Unstable, undependable.

top Possess.

chrysolite Precious stone.

My husband? Emilia repeats this in astonishment, twice. She at last sees the full truth.

mocks with A mockery of.

honest, honest ... Before the full revelation of his villainy Iago gets his persistent epithet repeated.

filthy bargain i.e. Othello.

Peace, you were best You had better be quiet.

gull Dupe. Emilia's description is an accurate one.

charm Silence.

I thought so then This seems to be a reference to her suspicions, hitherto suppressed, when asked for the handkerchief.

uncle Procurer (slang). A 'niece' is therefore a whore.

thy father's dead This is the first we hear of Brabantio's death and the fact that it was brought on by Desdemona's marriage.

mortal to Killed.

thread i.e. of life.

turn Act.

curse ... side Dismiss his good angel.

reprobation Damnation.

the act of shame Sexual intercourse. Othello still refuses to accept the truth.

amorous works Love-making.

recognizance Token. Othello means the handkerchief.

Zounds See note on I, 1, 86.

Be wise ... Iago's threats to Emilia are one thing but when he tries to kill her he confirms his guilt.

coxcomb Fool.

stones Thunderbolts.

whipster Whipper-snapper. (See 'whisper', Act II Scene 1.)

honesty ... The complete irony of Othello's trust in Iago must strike the audience with the use of the often-repeated word in this context. Othello is asking what is the use of bothering about reputation if the virtue to which it should relate has gone. Compare this with Iago's words to Cassio II, 3, 258–268.

swan The swan was popularly supposed to sing just before death. Emilia echoes Desdemona's song. There is a cruel irony in this allusion to the falseness of men: Emilia has been betrayed utterly by her own husband.

the ice-brook's temper Spanish swords were much prized: they were strengthened by dipping the red-hot metal in icy water.

naked Unarmed.

this little arm ... Note the pathos as Othello remembers his days of glory in this moment of catastrophe.

Who can control his fate? This is the invariable fact recognized by Shakespearian tragic heroes before their deaths.

butt Target.

sea-mark Beacon.

lost Needless.

Man Aim.

he retires ... Othello pretends to be a coward to divert attention from what he means to do, i.e. kill himself.

wench i.e. Desdemona.

count Account, i.e. Judgment Day.

cold, cold This contrasts with his many earlier references to the supposed heat of Desdemona's desire.

That's he that was Othello ... Othello's old image of himself – masterful, direct, honest and successful, the loving warlike husband of Desdemona – has been obliterated. His sense of identity has gone.

fable i.e. that the devil has cloven feet. Othello now recognizes what Iago knew all along: that the Ensign was a kind of devil.

sense Feeling.

practice Plotting.

honourable murderer Oxymoron. See note on V, 2, 21.

imports Portends, foretells.

discontented paper Letter expressing discontent.

satisfied Killed.

Brave Provoke.

cast Dismissed.

Soft you ... Othello is calm again: as the end of this speech shows, he has reached his decision to die. Unlike the rather hysterical lines 260–65, this is a rational account, first of his past service, then of the catastrophe that has overtaken him.

unlucky This has a stronger sense than now: unfortunate, ill-omened.

Of one ... extreme A judicious account of Othello's character and predicament. Clear sight has returned to him.

wrought Involved in deceit.

perplex'd Distracted.

subdued Tamed.

in Aleppo ... It seems that Othello is about to embark on a story: his death comes as all the more of a shock. The incident described highlights his courage and loyalty.

period Climax.

I kiss'd ... a kiss The ideas of love and death, associated throughout the play, come together here in the final oxymoron: 'to die upon a kiss'.

This did I ... heart *Because* he was great of heart, *though* he had no weapon, as I thought: suicide was the only noble way out.

Spartan dog This may refer to Iago's cruel and unrelenting behaviour: in ancient Greece the Spartans were famous for their courage and endurance.

fell Cruel.

lodging i.e. what lodges in this bed – Desdemona and Othello, united in death on their marriage-bed.

object Sight.

succeed to Devolve on.

Revision questions on Act V

1 Analyse Othello's two soliloquies in this Act, paying attention to ways in which their style reflects the state of the hero's mind.

2 What is the significance of Iago's silence at the end of the play when seen in the context of his behaviour throughout?

3 Can we accept Emilia's conversion from cynicism to commitment at the end of the play? If so, on what grounds?

4 The action takes place at night. What is the importance of this?

5 What is there about the last Act which can be said to make *Othello* a tragedy?

Shakespeare's art in *Othello*

Setting

Critical theories in the sixteenth century demanded that a play should have three 'dramatic unities': action, place and time. The idea behind this was to preserve credibility. The drama was meant to deal with a single story in a single place, with the events occupying not more than twenty-four hours. Shakespeare was indifferent to the unities. While achieving unity of action in the tragedies by focusing on the fate of a central character, he usually complicates the action with sub-plots, stretches it over long periods of time, and moves about from place to place. The only exception to this is *The Tempest*.

In *Othello* we move from Venice to Cyprus. The places are not distinguished physically but there are symbolic differences, which become important in the play. The republic of Venice was ruled by a powerful council, of which Brabantio is a typical member. The Venetians were famously proud but also cosmopolitan, taking their wealth from international trade – hence the importance of Cyprus. As a black moor, Othello is an outsider in this white commercial society. In Cyprus, having saved that island from the Turks, he is an all-powerful hero – at least until the Venetian council replaces him with Cassio. Venice represents stability, order, authority, the conventional respectable world. Cyprus is the scene of war and intrigue, where Iago can hatch his plots and Othello's ascendancy be shown up for what it is: precarious and vulnerable. Venice is the place Lodovico goes back to at the play's end to report the strange events that have taken place in Cyprus. The two places become symbolic of order and disorder, stability and passion, continuing life and disaster.

Chronology

Shakespeare compresses Cinthio's leisurely story into three days (only two in Cyprus), in the interests of swiftness, power and unity of action.

The movement of the play is marked according to the following timetable.

Act I   Late at night.
         Journey to Cyprus off stage. Time indeterminate
Act II   First day in Cyprus, morning (till late at night)
Act III Second day in Cyprus (the early morning after the drunken-
         ness of Cassio).
Act IV   Second day (later)
Act V   Second day (late at night)

The student will probably be surprised on seeing the above timetable set out, for although swift when its time is analysed, the play is not so swift in its general impression. In Act II (after only one day in Cyprus) Roderigo's 'money is almost spent'. In Act III Emilia says that her wayward husband 'hath *a hundred times* woo'd' her to steal Desdemona's handkerchief – a hundred times in a few days, even allowing for the voyage from Venice! All the conversation between Iago and Othello about Desdemona implies that Othello and Desdemona have been married for some time. Iago says that he 'lay with Cassio lately'. In that case it must have been in Venice, for they were both on guard on the only night that they had spent in Cyprus. If it is a lie, Iago is cunning enough not to make his lie clash with obvious possibilities. Bianca is dissatisfied because Cassio has kept *a week* away from her, and Cassio says that he will strike off his 'score of absence'. In Act IV Roderigo complains, '*Every day* thou daffest me with some device, Iago . . . I will indeed *no longer* endure it'. In Act V Desdemona says to Othello, 'You are fatal then when your eyes roll so', as if she is used to it. And at the end Othello tells the people assembled that Desdemona 'with Cassio hath the act of shame *a thousand times* committed'.

Students should remember, however, that inconsistencies like this, which are noticed when one *reads* the play, comparing passage with passage, would go unnoticed by an audience in the theatre. Shakespeare constructed his plays without regard for details, but with much regard for their general pattern.

Themes

To ask what *Othello* is 'about' is not to ask a simple question. Few literary works of any interest confine themselves to one theme, but open out to interpretation. Shakespeare's ascendancy in European literature over the centuries has inevitably produced a great deal of this. On the other hand, it is helpful to identify groups or clusters of related themes about which people can agree.

Love and hatred are clearly central to the play: even more important, perhaps, is the relationship between them, the way in which one can lead to the other, the sense that they are sides of the same coin. Different kinds of love are explored in the play: husband and wife, mistress and maid; but the main area of interest is erotic, for it is here that love can easily turn to hatred, or to jealousy and suspicion. The nature of Desdemona's love is uncomplicated, but Othello's is scrutinized in depth under pressure. Associated with the theme of love and hatred are subsidiary themes of *trust, honour, loyalty, betrayal,* and the social, sexual and personal factors that complicate these. Iago is as much a focal point in this respect as are Othello and Desdemona.

These themes are all focused on the central betrayal of Othello by Iago, and the General's tragic downfall. Tragic fate itself constitutes a kind of theme: though enacted rather than directly discussed in the play, its moral and spiritual implications are made explicit. Man's ignorance of circumstances, fate and other men; his helplessness in the face of evil; the tragic consequences of pride: all these are themes of any tragedy, here explored in the concrete situation of Othello's love for Desdemona. Associated with these themes is the idea of the outsider, which has special relevance for this play. Both Othello and Iago are outsiders in different senses, and their isolation from the human community of the play – literal in Othello's case, moral and spiritual in Iago's – proves to be crucial. If Othello were not a stranger in Venice his insecurity would not react so disastrously upon his temper; if Iago had any notion of anything but the primacy of self-interest he might not act as he does. If even Desdemona were not herself so isolated from family and friends she might be spared her fate. The small number of characters in Othello emphasizes the sense of their apartness, each from the other. This is reinforced by threads of imagery running through the play connected with injury and betrayal, speech and silence, deception, savage beasts and devils, all of which point to the precariousness of life, its perplexity and its perils.

Othello *as a tragedy*

The classic description of what a tragedy should be occurs in the *Poetics* of Aristotle, a Greek philosopher of the fourth century BC. According to Aristotle, tragedy should feature a hero who is an intermediate sort of person – neither especially good nor especially bad – who passes from happiness to misery as a result not of vice or depravity but because of an error of judgement, which makes him the victim of circumstances beyond his control. Central to this description is the notion of ignorance – that the hero should be unaware of some vital knowledge that is revealed to him at the climax of the drama, precipitating his downfall. The purpose of tragedy is to inspire pity and terror in the audience and to purge or purify them by their witnessing of the spectacle.

Shakespeare was one of several playwrights in 17th-century England experimenting with tragedy, and he made a major contribution to the form corresponding with Aristotle at some points but not at others. While it is unlikely that Shakespeare knew anything of Aristotle directly, having little knowledge of the Greek language, he almost certainly would be familiar with the plays of Seneca (4 BC–AD 65), a Roman playwright whose versions of the Greek tragedies about which Aristotle wrote were immensely popular in the late sixteenth century.

Seneca's plays stress the violent aspects of tragedy: they are dark, gloomy and savage, with a great relish for extravagant, bloody language – all features observable in *Othello*. More important, though, was Seneca's transmission to Renaissance Europe of the tragic form, and this too we can see in *Othello*. Here the hero falls from prosperity to misery, just as Aristotle says he should; and his fall is the result of an error of judgement about Desdemona's nature and Iago's, which makes him vulnerable to circumstances beyond his control. Throughout most of the play he is in ignorance about Iago's plot and this is only revealed to him in the final climax of the play. Pity and terror, which Aristotle speaks of as producing the catharsis, or purgation, are certainly among the responses of the audience: pity for the fates of Othello and Desdemona, and terror at the horror they have just witnessed.

But there are also important differences from Aristotle's prescription, and these tell us a good deal about the characteristic mode of Shakespearian tragedy. For one thing, the *Poetics* demands a clear distinction between base and noble characters: the involvement of such a crude character as Emilia in the tragic fate of the protagonists is frowned upon because it detracts from the dignity of the action. Shakespeare likes to mix the various elements of his theatre, which classical theory said should be kept apart: comedy and tragedy; the serious and the absurd; lofty, average and low kinds of speech; jokes and disasters. Thus the character of Iago, inconceivable in classical tragedy, is at times humorous even in his wickedness. This mixing of the elements contributes to the sense of variety and richness in Shakespeare's work and – as in the case of Iago – can incomparably heighten the drama.

Another, more important, difference from Aristotle results from the emphasis Shakespeare puts on the psychological study of his characters. In the *Poetics* we are told that the essence of tragedy is action, and that character is a secondary consideration: what matter are the causal relationship of events and the unity of the action – the way in which the end is shown to be an inevitable result of the beginning. While *Othello* is one of Shakespeare's most concentrated and unified plays, action takes second place to character. To put it another way, the important action is internal rather than external: it goes on in the mind and soul of the hero.

Linked with this is Shakespeare's distinctive treatment of what the Greeks called *hubris*. *Hubris* is the pride of a man who forgets his human limitations, especially the limits of his knowledge. Ignorance is a theme of *Othello*, a play in which all the main characters disastrously lack sufficient insight into one another. No one knows the true Iago; Desdemona is ignorant of Othello's violent and suspicious nature; Othello shows by his jealousy that he does not truly understand his wife; Iago's failure to understand the nature of love and loyalty leads him to underestimate these qualities in his wife. In classical tragedy the main victim of *hubris* is the hero. In *Othello*, however, it is the villain who manifests this kind of pride most distinctively. While Othello can certainly be called proud in a way – the play's action savagely tames his pride – it is Iago who constantly boasts in his soliloquies about what a clever fellow he is, and how he is making fools of everyone else. It is by looking for a moment at the role of Iago that we shall see what an unusual, even unique tragedy *Othello* is.

Aristotle tells us that all the characters in a tragedy must be good if the audience are to sympathize with them. Iago is indisputably wicked. Furthermore, the usual formula decrees that the hero is brought low by a fault in his own nature which puts him in the grip of uncontrollable circumstances; but Othello is brought low by the human agency of Iago, not by the gods or by destiny. This has led some critics to suggest that Othello's fate is not really grand enough for a tragic hero, because he is pitted against a base individual, not against providence or the divine will. Others have seen the strange uncertainty about Iago's motivation – is he really jealous of Emilia and so upset about a missed promotion that never seemed likely? In this view Iago's lack of positive motivation – what Coleridge called his 'motiveless malignity' – appears as a sign that he is important in the play not as an individual but as the embodiment of a natural force: irrational, inexplicable evil. Certainly Iago's almost godlike power over Othello, Cassio and Roderigo suggests something more than the human, but perhaps the true explanation of the puzzle lies in the simple fact that this is, on the contrary, an entirely human tragedy with nothing divine about it.

This last point would answer another criticism: that the central theme of the play, Othello's love for Desdemona, is not sufficiently important as the basis of a tragedy. Classical critics took the view that sexual love was an insufficient motive for tragedy because it is an animal passion: tragedy, they thought, should deal with what is divine in man – his reason and his soul. *Othello* has been criticized adversely on just this basis: that all the passions in the play are crude and trivial. But here the general point about Shakespeare should be made. In both *Othello* and *Antony and Cleopatra* – two of his greatest tragedies – he makes sexual passion crucial to the play and to the hero's downfall because in both plays it is the nature of man, not the vengeance or ill-will of the gods, which produces the tragedy. In *Othello* Iago admits to his own devilish nature when he invokes the 'divinity of hell', and the play is full of references to heaven and hell. But heaven and hell are shown to exist on earth and the characters experience them in life. The agencies of fate do not descend from Olympus: they dwell in the minds of the protagonists.

The characters

Othello

My blood begins my safer guides to rule

There have been two traditional views about Othello's character. One, exemplified in the criticism of A. C. Bradley's *Prefaces to Shakespeare*, sees Othello as a noble hero, trapped by Iago's machinations in a web of deceit and misunderstanding. According to this view Iago exploits Othello's very virtues – courage, trustfulness, and the capacity for passionate commitment – so that they become the source of weakness. It is the same with Desdemona: her 'heavenly purity of heart' as Bradley calls it, ensures her downfall at the hands of the cunning Ensign. The other view of Othello, most famously expressed in the work of T. S. Eliot and F. R. Leavis, suggests that he is by no means a blameless victim, but a crude, vain egotist who deserves his fate: a man so in love with his self-image that he is incapable of loving Desdemona except as the projection of his own ideal. The slightest suspicion of that ideal – which is really a suspicion of himself – makes him easy prey for Iago.

There is a good deal to be said for both views, and while clearly opposed in their extremer forms – Othello cannot be both noble and vicious – the two are not necessarily mutually exclusive. The fact that they exist points to a central problem in the interpretation of the play, which results from its double centre. How can we talk about this play as a tragedy and Othello as the tragic hero, when it is Iago who initiates all the action and who holds the centre of the stage for so much of the time? Despite being a man of action by repute, Othello must strike us as essentially passive in the context of the play: he does not act, he reacts. Because such a lot depends upon the view we take of Othello's character, it is important to look closely at its presentation and development.

He first appears in Act I Scene 2, and at once dispels the image of him presented by Iago in the previous scene. Here is no ill-judging, lecherous boor, but a decisive, dignified and proud man: 'I fetch my life and being/From men of royal siege' he says (I, 2, 21–2), asserting that he is as good as any man. Pride is an important element in his make-up. Not only is he proud of his ancestry and military success: his subsequent development makes sense only in relation to a declared pride in frankness and openness of character: 'My parts, my title, and my perfect soul/ Shall manifest me rightly' (I, 2, 31–2). When he says this we are clearly meant to admire him and we do, for this is a judgement echoed by the other characters – even Iago, who admits to Othello's 'free and noble nature' and his 'constant, loving, noble nature.' Desdemona, too, remarks that she saw Othello's 'visage in his mind,' and believes almost to the end that he could never stoop to the baseness of suspicion. What may worry the audience at this point in the play is that Othello so clearly admires himself for his frankness, which he mentions several times in the first Act, telling the duke and senators, for example, that 'Rude am I in my speech . . .' (I, 3, 81). Othello is neither an observant nor a subtle man: he doesn't notice things in others, such as Iago's fawning and Desdemona's evident loyalty. He misses things in himself, failing to distinguish between legitimate self-esteem and overweening pride. This distinction is important, for it is his pride, making up so large a part in his image of himself, which is humbled by the disaster, and which parallels Iago's very different pride in his ability to control events. Throughout the play the two act as distorted reflections of each other. They both deceive themselves, Iago about his power and Othello about his self-knowledge. When the general becomes a monster of jealousy we see that he was wrong about his frankness: there are hidden and frightening depths to his personality.

Othello's pride should not blind us, however, to his real qualities. In Act I Scene 2 he immediately quells a brawl with a few words: 'Keep up your bright swords, for the dew will rust 'em . . .' and we recognize his natural authority. He is both incisive and eloquent. While we would naturally expect depths of self-revelation in a Shakespearian hero as part of the playwright's artistry, in Othello's case references to his inability to handle words highlight the fact that he *can* handle them. This in turn shows us that his actual character does not correspond entirely with the image he likes to present of it. He shows confidence in the face of Brabantio's charges of witchcraft and is undismayed by the hostility of this former friend.

On the other hand, the long speeches in which he describes

and explains his marriage to Desdemona (I, 3, 76–170) reveal egotism and even vanity. Othello does not apologize to the man (Brabantio) who formerly treated him so well, and shows no signs of flinching at the contemptuous suggestion that Desdemona would never have married a black man were she in her senses. He almost presents the courtship as a matter of Desdemona's wooing, not his own. We must be careful not to overstress points Shakespeare has neglected in the interests of making his main point in this speech, i.e. the passionate, lofty, and far from lecherous nature of Othello's love for Desdemona. On the other hand the impression of egotism is borne out later in the play, notably in his obsessive references to the way his wife has betrayed *his* honour and *his* position and *his* happiness, in Act IV. She has made him, he says, 'A fixed figure, for the time of scorn/To point his slow unmoving fingers at . . .' (IV, 2, 55–6). His wavering resolve to kill her in Act V refers not to her as a person but to the impression she makes on *him*. Othello is a selfish, self-centred man.

In Act I all this is in the future. Because we recognize in Othello at the start of the play a striking character, effortless authority, and the admiration or submission of the other characters, we may be inclined to excuse his faults as minor. It is only when they come under the severe stress generated by his suspicion that they become crucial. In this respect Othello is a traditional tragic hero: one who falls from prosperity to adversity through the impact of unavoidable circumstances on a flaw in his judgement. Shakespeare is at pains to establish Othello's blackness in the text – Iago refers to it several times in the first scene – because it marks him as an outsider: a negro among white men, a Moor among Venetians, a professional soldier among courtiers and merchants. His pride is a natural compensation for this, but Iago is able to play on it when he suggests that Brabantio was right in saying that no white girl in her senses would marry a black man (III, 3, 233). The blackness that so magnificently marks Othello out becomes, in time, the sign of his isolation, and it works to strange effect in the pattern of this play, which is so often marked by reversals of the expected. Thus the noble and virtuous hero is black, the villain white. Early in the play, the black Othello is seen as positive, life-giving and dominant; the white Iago gradually emerges as negative and murderous. At the beginning of the play Othello specifically repudiates the dark powers of witchcraft (I, 2, 169), which he later attributes to the handkerchief, when he has come under the Ensign's spell.

In Act II Othello is at a high point in both love and war. Just as Act I Scene 2 features news of a wedding interrupting a council of war, so Act II Scene 1 gives us triumphant love and military victory. The close relationship of the themes of love and war dates back in Western literature to Homer's *Iliad*, and the two ironically counterpoint each other with images of sexual and soldierly battle, conflict, victory and submission. While the two themes are not causally connected in *Othello*, it is vital to take account of the fact that the hero is a soldier, not only in occupation but in his whole attitude to life. Like Iago, he is fond of presenting himself as a plain, straightforward man – a presentation which, in both cases, appears more and more ironic as the play progresses and Othello sinks into a morass of introspection while his lieutenant weaves more and more devious schemes. Yet his self-image remains a soldierly one, and this is justified by what we know of his success in war and the high esteem in which the Venetians hold him on this account; '. . . opinion . . . throws a more safer voice on you . . .' he is told by the Duke (I, 3, 225) when appointing him to command the fleet – though Othello's victory over the Turks takes on a certain hollowness, having been achieved through the good offices of a fortunate storm. This puts the very slightest cloud on the horizon of his relationship with Desdemona in Act II. Luck, in the shape of prosperity or good fortune, is essential to the hero: when it deserts him he becomes tragic. Up to Act II Scene 1 Othello is a fortunate man; after that his love for Desdemona is poisoned and his soldierly character destroyed. Iago makes this point most cruelly when he taunts Othello, in the midst of his suffering; with the words, 'Would you would bear your fortunes like a man!' (IV, 1, 61). This is the worst insult he could offer to the virile Othello's image of himself. Yet he is right; the Moor's virtues of courage and steadfastness have by then disappeared in hysterical jealousy. Only at the end of the play do they make a chastened reappearance. Even then his suicide is ambiguous. Is it the courageous exit of a soldier, or the despairing escape of a broken man? Perhaps both.

One of the play's many ironies, brought out by juxtaposing the military and erotic themes, results from the fact that it is

Othello's love which makes him vulnerable to Iago, and thus turns him from a brave soldier into a half-crazed neurotic. Love of a woman destroys his love of honour even as he thinks he is preserving his honour, for his suspicion makes him stoop to spying and eavesdropping. On the other hand, it is love which brings forth his most magnificent poetry, both before the murder of his wife and after. When, for example, he enters in Act II Scene 1, the whole tone of the play alters from worldly banter to exalted lyrical fervour: 'It gives me wonder great as my content/ To see you here before me . . .' he says (II, 1, 183), balancing wonder and content as the two things his love combines. By the end of the play these have been replaced by suspicion and discontent: 'Yet she must die, else she'll betray more men . . .' (V, 2, 6). We watch this change occurring most closely in Act III, Scene 3, in which we also see the peculiar combination of qualities in Othello's nature which prove his downfall. Put briefly, he is both volatile and stubborn: he is susceptible to influence and suspicion, but once his mind has hold of an idea he clings to it and lets it grow. In Act III Scene 3 the two characteristics begin to conflict violently as one idea – that of Desdemona's guilt – struggles with another – Desdemona's innocence – for mastery in his mind: 'I think my wife be honest, and think she is not,/I think that thou art just, and think thou art not . . .' (III, 3, 390–91). This is why he craves certainty to relieve him from the pain of conflict. During this scene Iago gradually converts him from irritable doubt to savage belief in his wife's infidelity; and it is in this scene that Othello's critical weaknesses are revealed and the question of his heroic status is most poignantly raised. For he is shown to be emotionally unstable, pathologically suspicious, and even petty.

It is also in Act III Scene 3 that the complexity of Othello's relationship with Iago is fully developed, running sinisterly in parallel with his relationship to his wife. As one waxes the other wanes. Powerful hints of erotic imagery at the final climax of this very long scene suggest that Desdemona has been replaced as Othello's partner by Iago in a demonic parody of the marriage ceremony. The two men kneel. Othello speaks of 'the due reverence of a sacred vow', and Iago responds by promising to 'obey' his master, ending the scene with the words 'I am your own for ever' (III, 3, 467–486). Even the language – reverence, obey, love – hints at a kind of matrimony. This incident underlines the powerful motivating force of sexual love and jealousy in the play, reminds us of Iago's obsession with sexuality and hints at a kind of erotic bond between the two men. That is not to say there is a homosexual attraction between them, though the play has sometimes been performed in this spirit, presenting Iago in terms of a frustrated passion for Othello. On the other hand, Shakespeare is fascinated by magnetic male characters whose combination of strength and weakness exerts a strong attraction on those around them: Othello, Coriolanus and Antony all belong in this mould. All three men think of themselves as simple characters and are in fact complex. This ultimately contributes to their self-destruction. They are men of one idea.

After Act III Scene 3 Othello does not develop: he deteriorates. Only in the closing moments of the play is this process reversed, when the conflict within Othello, born out of jealousy, has been momentarily resolved by the murder of Desdemona and then horribly reawakened by the revelation of Iago's treachery, producing a vision of hell: 'Blow me about in winds, roast me in sulphur,/Wash me in steep-down gulfs of liquid fire!' (V, 2, 280–81).

Only at the very end does Othello regain some of his self-possession, but now his pride has been savagely tempered by experience. Like Hamlet and Lear, he realizes too late that to take the gifts of fortune for a sign of personal merit is to presume beyond the proper limits of human knowledge. Thus at the end of the play it seems that Othello does indeed combine features of both those critical views we noted at the beginning of this account: he is both heroic and weak, loving and cruel, steadfast and volatile. Contradiction is a fundamental principle in the understanding of his character.

Iago

I am not what I am.

The idea of self-deception provides a useful key to Iago's character, leading to his crucial role in the development of the plot and producing much of the play's irony. It is self-deception that creates the apparent complexity of Iago's character. Othello is distinguished by noble simplicity in the first part of the play; in contrast, Iago's behaviour seems intricate and devious, until we realize that it results from his failure to understand himself and his own deserts. At the beginning of the play he describes his own approach to life as 'throwing but shows of service' (I, 1, 52), but when he says later in the same speech that 'I am not what I am' (I, 1, 65) the disturbing paradox in the phrase (how can he be what he is not?) suggests not only deception of others but of Iago's self. His pride in trickery blinds him to the fact – exposed at the end of the play – that no one can fool all the people all the time: to believe that one can is to fool oneself. Iago's refusal to speak in the last scene:

Demand me nothing, what you know, you know,
From this time forth I never will speak word. (V, 2, 304–5)

shows this manipulator of verbal fictions hoist with his own petard: silence is his last form of deceit.

In fact Iago's cleverness is strictly of the limited variety. Apparently intelligent, witty, boisterous, obscene and sensible by turns, the Ensign is really none of these things, but an obsessive, vindictive, petty and arrogant scoundrel, who is at least right about one thing: his various qualities are indeed only shows. None of them represents the 'real' Iago whose reality is entirely negative: it lives only in destruction. He encompasses the downfall of larger, grander spirits than himself. Presented to the world as a bluff professional soldier, full of *bonhomie*, Iago reveals in his soliloquies the self-image of the cynical master plotter: 'My medicine, work: thus credulous fools are caught...' (IV, 1, 45). Yet neither the public nor the private man corresponds to what the audience learn about this emotional, impulsive and sometimes frightened egotist – one so consumed by his minor grievances, that he not only loses all sense of proportion about them, but grotesquely overrates his own merit and degree of self-awareness. The grievances become irrelevant to his true desire: the exercise of power over better men than himself.

Iago is guilty of pride, a fault usually said to be characteristic of the tragic hero. This is not to say that he should displace Othello in the title of the play: several Shakespeare tragedies (e.g. *Macbeth* and *Antony and Cleopatra*) feature a hero brought to disaster through the agency of an unscrupulous, persuasive companion. The point here is that while Iago has pride he lacks tragic stature and sympathy. Whatever their faults, Othello, Macbeth and Antony have large natures to which we can respond: they have virtues as well as vices; they are foolish but not mean; in the last analysis they face things out and accept the consequences. Their accomplices escape into silence or suicide. While in each case the fate of the secondary character reflects that of the hero, it is lacking in exposed grandeur.

Iago's basic principle is self-interest: 'In following him, I follow but myself (I, 1, 58)', he says of Othello at the beginning of the play, reiterating this sentiment in different forms throughout. He advises others to do the same. 'Put money in thy purse' he tells Roderigo (I, 3, 340), later seeming to advise Cassio to plead with Desdemona out of the kindness of his heart: 'I think you think I love you' (II, 3, 302). In both cases the advice is ironic, for Iago is bending the two men to his own will and involving them in disaster. Iago's cunning selfishness is not unusual in the drama of Shakespeare's time: the demonic villain, with neither principle nor pity, appears in plays by Christopher Marlowe and John Webster. But Shakespeare's character is unusual in the depth and detail of his portrayal; the psychological penetration of his self-deception; the strange complexity of his relationship to Othello; and the powerful sense we have of the ultimate mystery at the heart of his nature. In the end Iago's evil is inexplicable: there is no proportion between the scale of his grievances and the scale of his revenge. He is simply 'like that'. His self-interest is shown to be not only short-sighted in the long term but far from the calculated strategy he presents to himself. Iago is a great improviser. Note the way he is able to turn Roderigo's anger against himself, to positive effect (IV, 2, 175–244). But by assuming that men are fools if they do not act from self-interest, he disastrously fails to allow for the nobler motives of honour, truthfulness and love. This is made ironically clear at the end of the play when Emilia – the person he has counted on for blind obedience to his will – rises up against him: 'I'll be in speaking, liberal as the air' she says (V, 2, 221), demonstrating that, for all her declared cynicism, her better feelings can prevail over loyalty to a husband whose villainy she has at last completely perceived. This moment encapsulates the depth of Iago's self-deception: too impressed by his own schemes, clever enough to dispose of Roderigo, a witness to his evil-doing, he forgets about his own wife.

Iago's situation is ironic through and through because he depends on fooling others while he is himself fooled about the extent of his own powers. In striving to dominate others he is betrayed by his own base passions; he brings about their downfall only at the cost of his own. This irony is revealed time and time again in his speeches, especially in the soliloquies where he boasts of his knowledge of human nature. 'Thus do I ever make my fool my purse' (I, 3, 381), he says of Roderigo, forgetting that the main person to be tortured by these thoughts is Iago himself, even though he admits to being a kind of devil:

> Divinity of hell!
> When devils will their blackest sins put on,
> They do suggest at first with heavenly shows,
> As I do now . . . (II, 3, 341–4)

In the same speech he shows a clear perception of Desdemona's nature, understanding that this makes her especially vulnerable:

> For 'tis most easy
> The inclining Desdemona to subdue,
> In any honest suit; she's fram'd as fruitful
> As the free elements . . . (II, 3, 330–3)

Yet the hatred and vile bitterness Iago displays ('So will I turn her virtue into pitch') show him to be living in a kind of hell. Devilish images are associated with him throughout. At the very end of the play Lodovico calls him a 'hellish villain' (V, 2, 369), but this is no worse than the names he gives himself. At this stage, however, he is to be consigned to the real hell in two senses: physical torture, and life after death. He thus accurately but unknowingly predicts his own fate.

Desdemona

She was in love, and he she lov'd prov'd mad.

There is a sense in which Desdemona's character has less importance than her role: what she represents in relation to Othello and Iago matters more than what she is. This is largely because her character is not presented in the same depth and detail as theirs. The name Desdemona means 'unhappy' – a word that describes her fate better than it describes her nature, which is patient and sweet-tempered but by no means passive.

Desdemona's character, like Othello's, has been the subject of critical dispute. Is she a virtuous and helpless victim of circumstances or a forward hussy who brings about her own demise and the general catastrophe at the end of the play? Perhaps it is necessary to remind ourselves of two points when thinking about Desdemona: first, that we cannot expect a character in a play to have the same sort of coherence we attribute to people in life; second, that the coherence we attribute to people in life is often itself a cover for contradictions and complexities beyond our comprehension. In drama there are times when behaviour may seem to be 'out of character' but may make sense in the context of the play as a whole.

The crux of the critical dispute about Desdemona concerns Act II Scene 1, in which the reputedly shy and 'innocent wife exchanges coarse witticisms with Iago for almost eighty lines (II, 1, 100–79). This passage appears to contradict Brabantio's description of his daughter as

> A maiden never bold of spirit,
> So still and quiet, that her motion
> Blush'd at her self . . . (I, 3, 94–6)

Yet this apparent contradiction tells us a good deal about Desdemona. The point here is that we must not confuse purity with either ignorance or simplicity. Desdemona is pure, not in the sense that she has never thought about sex or had sexual feelings – as Brabantio implies – but because, unlike Othello and Iago, she does not become obsessed with sexuality, or cynically undervalue it like Emilia. Having once chosen Othello for her husband she is also completely faithful to him and is clearly and consciously able to locate her sexual relationship with him in the larger context of the other demands marriage makes and the other kinds of happiness it has to offer. She makes this point quite explicitly in I, 3, 248–59, when she explains that she does not want to be parted from Othello, but to live with him as his wife in every sense – including, of course, the sexual sense – because she is devoted to him, physically and mentally. It is in this spirit that Othello replies and echoes her (I, 3, 260–74). But while Othello changes his view of this, becoming obsessed, through Iago's agency, with the sexual aspect of marriage, Desdemona maintains her balanced view – a considerable irony in the light of Othello's suspicions. When we take this idea of Desdemona's purity into account, II, 1, 100–79 becomes comprehensible: Desdemona, from a wealthy background, is well able to handle the kind of crude flirtation common in such

16th-century households. The dominant element of word-play in the passage makes it quite clear that the whole thing is indeed a matter of words, not of feelings or attitudes. These are the most conventional platitudes they are exchanging, in a matter of courtesy to which Desdemona feels bound in her role as the General's wife entertaining his subordinates. She *shows* as little anxiety as possible for her husband's welfare – while making her private feelings clear in the question 'there's one gone to the harbour?' and her statement that she is pretending to be other than she really is: 'I do beguile/The thing I am, by seeming otherwise . . .' (II, 1, 122–3).

If we now look at that part of the play in which we first meet Desdemona (Act I Scene 3) we can see that before she actually appears she has been seriously misrepresented in two different, and indeed opposite, ways. First Iago paints her as no better than a prostitute, and a good deal worse: indulging in sexual excess not for money but for sheer lust. Then Brabantio goes to the other extreme, claiming a particular innocence for her, as we have seen, in Act I Scene 3. Both men are making out cases in which Desdemona is a mere instrument; both are attempting to blacken Othello's name. But when Desdemona comes on to the stage she shows no sign of either lechery or neurotic shyness; like Othello himself, she is quiet, self possessed, confident and articulate. This is no silly headstrong girl: she has a grasp of the issues: 'I do perceive here a divided duty . . .' (I, 3, 181), and the ability to sort them out: 'I am hitherto your daughter: but here's my husband . . .' (I, 3, 185). She shows no fear of Brabantio at this point, just as she is quite confident of tackling Othello on Cassio's behalf later in the play.

If we refrain from making the mistaken equation between purity and innocence on the one hand and naiveté and unsophistication on the other, Desdemona's character and its importance in the play become clear: impressed as she is by Othello, both on his testimony and her own, she feels herself capable of coping with the delicate situation in which marriage with an older man of another colour from a different culture will plunge her – a confidence revealed in her intercessions for Cassio. This confidence is her undoing, for she knows nothing of Othello's weaker side, and it is one of the play's most distinct ironies that while he suspects her of having a sexual weakness it is precisely her lack of suspicion that he himself is susceptible when it comes to matters of sexual passion, which helps to prove their mutual undoing. Like everyone else in this play, Desdemona is guilty of misunderstanding, or rather of having insufficient knowledge; she does not know enough about the darker side of the human heart until it is too late.

Only at the end of the play does she, like Othello, come to some insight about what is the matter, but unlike Othello Desdemona does not change as a result of this knowledge. On the contrary, the final testimony to her strength of character is the extent to which she remains constant to herself and her image of the world expressed in her idea of Othello. Thus her last words, in reply to Emilia's question about who has killed her, are not merely a ridiculous and melodramatic finale – though one may question Shakespeare's wisdom in having her seem to die, then revive, then die again. She says

Nobody, I myself, farewell:
Commend me to my kind lord, O, farewell! (V, 2, 125–6)

and in these words she blames both her own inadequacy and circumstances ('Nobody') for the catastrophe, but not Othello himself, whom she specifically exonerates in her last line: 'my kind lord' – for Desdemona is quite without irony, in a thoroughly ironic play. This acceptance of responsibility and her hint that the tragedy is in the nature of things is in stark contrast to Othello's own pitiable, if temporary, attempts to evade responsibility for the murder – as it is radically different from the inclination of all the other main characters – Cassio, Roderigo, Iago and Emilia – to escape the consequences of their actions. Even Othello's suicide and Iago's silence are forms of evasion: only Desdemona, apart from her very understandable fear of death itself ('Kill me tomorrow') faces up to things at the end of the play – as she did at the beginning when calmly stating the reasons for her marriage and her disinclination to go on living with her father.

Thus it is that the contradictions in Desdemona's character reveal a complex fictional person. Unlike Othello she is perceptive and responsive to others: sympathetic when he has a headache, interested in Emilia's opinions, sorry for Cassio. She is sensitive – 'A child to chiding' – and yet tactful: she refrains from contradicting her husband. Only when pressing Cassio's case does she seriously misunderstand the situation, and this is a case not for perception or sensitivity: it is a matter of absolutely fundamental incomprehension: Desdemona simply cannot see the darker side of Othello. This incomprehension is echoed throughout the play in Othello's misreading of his wife Desdemona, Emilia's failure to know the depths of her husband's depravity, and everyone's misplaced trust in Iago. Thus Desdemona's failure to comprehend her husband – whom she hardly knows – is not so much a lack in her as a truth about human nature: that not only can we never know others completely, but that it may be their vital side which is concealed from us, however close we are to them. By behaving with absolute honour Desdemona does all she can: it is not within her power to penetrate evil or to change in her husband something of which she has no knowledge. Desdemona is no more the scheming minx of some critical views than she is the saint of A. C. Bradley: she is the dramatic respresentation of a young woman with virtues and limitations, of no malice, some humour and steadfastness, and a cruel fate.

Within the context of the whole play Desdemona, like Othello, is isolated. In common with the general run of Shakespearian heroines she has no mother, she is a solitary child, a girl torn between her father and her husband. In making her choice between them she gives the same reason as that other motherless girl Cordelia: that just as her mother left home to marry, so must she. Her isolation, like Othello's, throws her situation into sharp relief, intensified as it is by marrying out of her caste, increasing the pathos, emphasizing both her courage and her vulnerability – contrasts that are further heightened when we compare Desdemona with the two other women in the play: Emilia and Bianca.

Bianca

> 'tis the strumpet's plague
> To beguile many, and be beguiled by one.

Bianca's role, while minor in terms of the plot, is important in developing the play's themes. Of the three women in *Othello* she is socially and morally the most inconsiderable. Conceptually, however, given that much of the action and dialogue revolve around the sexuality of women, she has more significance.

Bianca is a prostitute; she lives by exploiting the physical desires of men. Paradoxically a prostitute is despised — and Bianca is no exception — not because she has base needs of her own but because she satisfies those of others. She is an appropriate character for a play that constantly illuminates the reversal of normal expectations and shows up the paradoxes of human passions, for Bianca's trade depends on the exclusion of love — that force which, in normal circumstances, is what makes sexual desire respectable and acceptable. The prostitute and her customers must conduct their dealings on a purely physical level. It is even more paradoxical, therefore, when Bianca becomes yet more subject to contempt because she foolishly falls in love with Cassio. Both Cassio and Iago despise her for this. In Act IV Scene 1 Iago comments on:

> the strumpet's plague
> To beguile many, and be beguil'd by one (lines 96–7)

and Cassio merely laughs when he and Iago discuss Bianca's passion. Bianca, on the other hand, is jealous when she concludes that the handkerchief Cassio has given her to copy — a thoroughly cruel thing for him to do — belongs to another of his girlfriends: 'Let the devil and his dam haunt you' (IV, 1, 146), she says to Cassio, and the audience may note the echoes of Othello, the play's other jealous lover, haunted by the devilish Iago. On another level Bianca's passion for Cassio — who uses her without returning her love — parallels Roderigo's unrequited love for Desdemona, making it ironically appropriate that Cassio and Desdemona should be paired in imagination by Iago. On her own social level and in her own way, Bianca comes very near to being exploited by Iago as he exploits Roderigo: after the attack on Cassio in V, 1 Iago implies that Bianca was involved. By this time he has already killed Roderigo and is looking for another scapegoat; his instinct is to use the sexual desire of others to get them into trouble. Bianca escapes only because Iago's plot is uncovered. But note that at the end of V, 1 Emilia is ready to believe Iago's hint — a point that reflects ironically back on the worldly-wise advice Emilia has been giving Desdemona about the rights of women in IV, 3. When it comes to the crunch, Emilia is ready to take the hypocritical male view of a prostitute's likely behaviour — especially unfair when Bianca's passion for Cassio is agreed to be the only sentimental commitment in her life. But if we can compare Bianca in different ways with the male characters, it is of course in relation to Emilia and Desdemona that she is mainly significant.

Desdemona, Emilia and Bianca can be seen as embodying different aspects of female sexuality: the responsible, the cynical and the economic. For Bianca sex is a commodity that she sells, and we can relate this fact to the way in which Roderigo and Iago constantly talk in terms of sexual gratification as a commodity that can be bought if there is enough money available. Even Othello is converted to this view. Bianca, then, represents what these men come to believe all women to be: a seller of wares. This is a notion from which Desdemona literally recoils in disgust when she says: 'I cannot say "whore":/It does abhor me now I speak the word' (IV, 2, 163), and which Emilia also rejects on the very different grounds that promiscuous women are only doing what men do, which legitimizes their behaviour. Yet even Bianca herself, as her passion for Cassio shows, has other ideas of love and sex than this: as a prostitute she is made in the image of male desire, which is the image that possesses and destroys Othello – the image of women as willing servants of male sexuality. It is this image that Iago consistently broadcasts, with his frequent references to the well-known lewdness of Venetian women. It is this image Iago is able to hint at when accusing Bianca of participating in the attack on Cassio, because of the associated notion that a woman will do anything to gratify her desires, and anything to revenge them if frustrated. Bianca embodies Othello's suspicions of Desdemona: what Bianca is, Desdemona may be. It is therefore fitting that in Act IV Scene 1 Othello mistakes the subject of a conversation between Iago and Cassio, taking it to be Desdemona they are talking about when it is in fact Bianca. In this scene both Othello and Cassio are betrayed by their attitude towards women, Othello by his suspicion and Cassio by his contempt. For Bianca serves also to mark the way in which men idealize some women and despise others, mistaking the reality in both cases: Desdemona is no more an angel than Bianca a devil, they are only thus as male desires would see them. The coincidence of Bianca's entry at this point (IV, 1, 142) is fitting: it makes Othello's mistake complete and deepens the irony of the confusion.

Emilia

I will not charm my tongue, I am bound to speak . . .

Emilia's importance is confined to the second part of the play, when she is instrumental in two vital incidents leading to Othello's downfall: the stealing of the handkerchief and the revelation of Iago's deceit. Yet she has a significance beyond this participation in the plot by virtue of the foil she provides to Desdemona and the attitude to life she embodies and expresses.

Emilia is both Iago's wife and Desdemona's maid, and a good deal hinges on this double role. As maids commonly do in Shakespeare, she expresses a no-nonsense approach to things in general and men in particular, in marked contrast to her mistress's views, but in harmony with the publicly expressed cynicism of Iago. One difference between them is that we understand Emilia to be expressing what she really believes to be her views – though these are transcended in the horrors of the play's last scene – whereas in her husband's case we can often not be sure that the cynical tone is not merely one more false face presented to the world. The other difference is that Emilia's opinions are offered with little theoretical basis, and without the sense we get from Iago that some neurosis or seriously damaging experience has helped to form them.

Emilia says what she thinks without much evidence of thought, and the quintessence of her views is given in Act IV Scene 3 when she is discussing men and marriage with her mistress. Her proclamation that women should: 'Let husbands know,/That wives have sense like them' (IV, 3, 93–4) would seem to complement and even offer justification for the low view Iago and then Othello have formed of women, if it were not for the fact that Emilia is simply claiming equality and right of reply: just as men have faults and frailties, she says, so have women, and that's all there is to it. Emilia's world revolves around practicalities: it is quite lacking in the moral and emotional imperatives that drive on Othello and Desdemona. And it is quite inadequate, as her stealing of the handkerchief shows: in a play that turns on such small things, these not only matter in themselves – motivating the plot as they do – they also provide a moral index to the characters. Emilia's failure to wonder why Iago wants the handkerchief at all, 'I nothing know but for his fantasy', and her consequent need to lie about it to Desdemona, show very clearly what is wrong with her attitude to life: Emilia's insistence on a practical approach to things proves as disastrous as the more important characters' absorption in higher concerns. And Emilia remains unaware, after purloining the handkerchief, that she has been in the presence of a moral dilemma about whether to be loyal to her mistress or to obey her husband. The fact that she refuses to speculate on why he should want the handkerchief shows her unease, however, indicating that beneath the pragmatism she does have a moral sense. It is this moral sense, of outraged decency and loyalty to her dead mistress, which makes her rebel in the end – again unthinkingly – against her husband, and pay for that rebellion with her life.

If Emilia is crude, she is not bad. Her sins are those of omission. Her part in unmasking Iago illustrates this point. So astounded is she by Othello's news – that Iago told him Desdemona was false – she cannot at first take it in, repeating the words 'My husband' three times, both as an uncomprehending question and a horrified confirmation: 'I thought so then' (V, 2, 193), she says, admitting that she has already suspected her husband of some treachery without being able to formulate what it was, but has suppressed the suspicion. To some extent this is a failure of understanding: Emilia parallels Desdemona in that she has not grasped the horrors of which her husband is capable, though she has not the excuse of Desdemona's inexperience. Emilia's claims to worldly wisdom are nullified by this failure. But once again the point is made that our knowledge of others is severely limited, and this limitation throws doubts on all the wisdom proffered in the play by the duke and others, Emilia included. The only true knowledge, it seems, comes from experience, usually when it is too late – at least for the participants in this drama. At this point Emilia finds that she *must* speak.

Cassio

He hath a daily beauty in life . . .

Like other characters in this play Cassio is the subject of contradictory reports. This process begins in Act I Scene 1, when Iago describes Othello and Cassio to Roderigo. To the Ensign Cassio is a man of no practical experience, having only theoretical knowledge of war, though the charge is meant to reflect more significantly on the quality of Othello's judgement than on Cassio himself. As the play progresses, however, Iago finds other reasons for disliking him – reminding us, incidentally, that jealousy is not restricted in this play to Othello. These reasons are more closely connected with the play's preoccupations. For Cassio is 'a proper man': good-looking and well set up; he is 'handsome, young and hath all those requisites in him that folly and green minds look after'. More specifically, Cassio is favoured by the three women in the play in their various ways. Bianca is in love with him, Desdemona intercedes in his favour, and Emilia is generally sympathetic in the manner of one who takes an interest in the fortunes of attractive young men. More-over, we learn at the beginning that Cassio is 'A fellow almost damn'd in a fair wife' (I, 1, 21), though she is never mentioned again, and Shakespeare concentrates on his actual sexual rela-tionship with Bianca and his supposed one with Desdemona.

In short, Cassio makes Iago feel inadequate. He is more attractive sexually – 'he hath a daily beauty in his life' – and he has been preferred in the matter of promotion by Othello – though we are never sure whether Iago's aspirations to the lieutenancy are even remotely justified. Besides, Cassio is not only Othello's subordinate, he is also a friend, and appears to belong to a more exclusive social set than Iago. Add to this that he is a Florentine and an educated man and he is a perfect target for Iago's hatred – more so, one might think, than Othello. But then, Othello and Cassio are both outsiders in Venetian society who have achieved more than the insider Iago, first in love and now in professional advancement. While admitting Cassio's advantages, Iago is therefore inclined either to belittle these – Cassio's superior education is the object of much scorn – or to make them reasons for his revenge.

It is right that the play should begin with Iago's complaints about Cassio, for the two characters are linked throughout. As the men most closely associated with Othello, they naturally invite comparison – an invitation to which Iago, at least, responds; Cassio is far too preoccupied with himself to think much about the Ensign. At first sight Cassio appears to have none of Iago's faults: his admiration for Othello is real; he says what he means; he reveals his true character without reserve (for example in the moments after Othello has dismissed him from the lieutenancy when Iago comforts him), he is polite and gracious, even excessively elaborate in his speech mannerisms; he adopts an attitude towards Desdemona with which the audience can identify; he is charming to everyone except Bianca; and has a touching faith in the evil Iago.

Iago, on the other hand, freely admits his intellectual and social inferiority to Cassio: indeed he makes it the basis of his claim to *superiority*, painting himself as a plain honest man in contrast with the urbane Cassio. But Iago also has a nose for other people's weaknesses, and he sniffs out two foibles of Cassio's which make us begin to think that the man is not such a paragon after all. The first is an excusably weak head: Cassio cannot take his alcohol. But we may conclude that this should make him all the more careful not to drink, whatever the social pressures, and the way in which he bows to Iago's insistence that he have just another is an indication of fundamental weakness. Not only does Cassio have a weaker head: Iago has a stronger will. When the damage is done Cassio's second foible shows up: his embarrassing anxiety to stand well with Othello, and inability to keep his shame to himself, reinforce the impression of weakness which contrasts sharply with Iago's steadfastness in his evil purpose. In this context even Iago's ability to dissemble seems to have a strength lacking in the over-talkative Cassio, all too ready to give himself away. These 'weaknesses' of course only take on significance in the extreme circumstances of the play: in a different place and a different time, Cassio would muddle through life quite happily.

But what is the justification for the general approval of Cassio, beyond the superficial qualities listed in the last paragraph – charm, warmth, politeness and so on? Desdemona calls him valiant, Othello addresses the 'good Michael', others call him 'a proper man'. The evidence of his actions offers a different picture. He is quite unscrupulous about concealing from Othello the fact that he keeps a mistress because, he has the cheek to tell Bianca herself, he thinks it 'no addition, nor my wish/To have him see me woman'd . . .' (III, 4, 192–3). Nor is there any sign of him telling Desdemona about his affair. Furthermore his treatment of Bianca is contemptible: he exploits her weakness for him while making a joke of her with others. Cassio is inveterately garrulous and sycophantic: he greets Desdemona's arrival in Cyprus with such fulsome praise that Shakespeare hints at the absurdity of it by making Cassio himself refer to 'the quirks of

blazoning pens' and speak in the style known in the
sixteenth century as euphuistic, after *Euphues* by Lyly, written in
a ridiculously ornate manner. Later, in Act II Scene 3, he is
overzealous to please Othello:

Iago hath directed what to do:
But not withstanding with my personal eye
Will I look to it. (lines 4–6)

Then, when he has disgraced himself, Cassio ˙shows neither
dignity nor counsel. Later, applying to Desdemona to intercede
for him, he pesters her with florid speeches:

If my offence be of such mortal kind,
That neither service past, nor present sorrows,
Nor purpos'd merit in futurity,
Can ransom me in his love again . . . (III, 4, 112–15)

The monotonous rhythm, inflation and formal language of
these lines indicate the pompous streak in Cassio – especially if
we compare them with any part of Iago's lively soliloquies. Only
under the pressure of either shame (in II, 3) or horror (V, 2)
does Cassio depart from this formal style into rhythms that
reflect true feeling. Otherwise he cultivates a polished manner,
just as false in its way as Iago's various guises.

Cassio, in fact, conforms to one of the play's themes, traced
through the imagery – the theme of deceit and self-deceit. Like
Iago, he is not what he seems, though he has not Iago's guilt in
deliberate and malevolent deception. The disguise Cassio prac-
tises is the sort any of us might – just as any of us might be guilty
of Emilia's avoidance of darker thoughts. The point of tragedy is
that these faults only become overtly dangerous when sucked
into the larger orbit of natures such as Iago's and Othello's.

Roderigo

One that fills up the cry.

The significant point about Roderigo, in the context of the play
as a whole, is that he does not appear in the Cinthio story from
which Shakespeare took his plot: he is the playwright's own
creation. This means that Shakespeare had very positive purposes in view when he introduced Roderigo into the action, and
the character is moulded accordingly. Roderigo has little inde-
pendent life as an individual: on the other hand, he is important

both in forwarding the plot and in providing a stooge for Iago, whose point of view we can compare with Roderigo's.

At the very beginning of the play Roderigo is the first to speak, and his opening lines define the financial nature of the relationship – it can hardly be called friendship – between him and Iago who 'hast had my purse . . .' (I, 1, 2). The themes of self-interest and cynical relationships with others, contrasted so sharply with Desdemona's love of Othello, are thus introduced at the play's outset. Roderigo is weak, rich and foolish: if the play did not develop into a tragedy, we might take it to be a comedy of the sort to which Ben Jonson, Shakespeare's great contemporary, was partial, about the fleecing of rich fools by rogues. The first scene of the play could well be performed as a sour farce in which Roderigo is quite dominated by Iago. He shows little individuality, his protests ('I take it much unkindly') are feeble, and he does as he is bidden without asking too many questions, presumably because he hopes that Iago will be grateful and take more trouble to further Roderigo's suit with Desdemona.

In terms of the dramatic presentation in the first scene, Roderigo is necessary as a confidant to whom Iago can unveil his plans for the audience's benefit. Iago, after all, is running unnecessary risks by taking someone into his confidence, when he might achieve the aim of upsetting Brabantio with an anonymous letter – but this would not offer the same opportunity for putting us in the picture. At this point Roderigo is necessary to the playwright, not as a character but as a dramatic device. Once Iago has taken Roderigo into his confidence, however, they become inevitable conspirators, and Roderigo is drawn into Iago's plot. We can judge the extent to which Shakespeare used him as a device by comparing Act I Scene 1, in which Brabantio tells Roderigo that 'I have charged thee, not to haunt about my doors' (line 96) with Act II Scene 1, in which it appears that Desdemona is quite unembarrassed to have travelled on the same ship as the man who formerly pestered her with his attentions: his role as the unwanted suitor is now over and Shakespeare abandons it without worrying too much about consistency, because Roderigo is necessary in Cyprus for another aspect of the plot, i.e. the conspiracy against Cassio.

Act I ends, as it began, with a long conversation between Roderigo and Iago, and these conversations are a feature of the play, occurring in Act I (1, 1–80 and 3, 301–80), Act II (1, 213–80 and 3, 354–72) Act IV (2, 174–244) and Act V (1, 1–7). Apart from the exchanges in Act V, which merely prepare the action, the others all provide a number of opportunities for Iago to elaborate his plot aloud; to show the quickness of his wit in satisfying Roderigo's dissatisfaction; to show him making a fool of Roderigo just as he takes in Othello; and to provide for the development of Iago's character. Each of the longer conversations is either preceded or followed by a soliloquy for Iago in which he reveals another level of his plans to which Roderigo is not privy, and which involve his deception. They are thus vital to the dramatic presentation of Iago, whose character is clearly distinguished from Roderigo's by his elaborate style: whereas Iago's conversation is full of complex images, rapid transitions from one idea to another and is highly 'theatrical', Roderigo speaks a simple prose, reflecting his dullness of mind and his complete lack of Iago's mercurial temperament. Furthermore their exchanges are always in prose: only Iago is given verse for his soliloquies.

Roderigo is not, however, a complete cipher. He understands that Desdemona is 'full of most blessed condition . . .' (II, 1, 247). He is prepared at times to do anything to achieve his aims – whether that means paying Iago large sums to further his suit with the general's wife, or committing murder which, at one stage, he prepares to do at Iago's bidding. Yet the ensign's ascendancy over him is not complete, for at the thought of murder, Roderigo has doubts: 'I have no great devotion to the deed' (V, 1, 7) he says, during his last conversation with Iago, though he still accepts the reasons his prompter has given. This suggests a weak character and intelligence, coloured both by the shadow of moral scruples and uncertainty about his capacity for resolute action: 'Be near at hand, I may miscarry in it' (V, 1, 6). At this point Iago decides that Roderigo must die, once he has performed the service of killing Cassio – in which context Roderigo's words, spoken a few seconds earlier: 'Tis but a man gone: forth, my sword he dies' take on both pathos and irony: Roderigo's indifference becomes his own downfall.

Like other characters in the play Roderigo is betrayed by circumstances beyond his knowledge and a failure to grasp the moral significance of truth and straight dealing. While admiring Desdemona for her 'most blessed condition' he cannot see the

inconsistency of attempting to win her by foul means: first black-
ening Othello's character and eventually agreeing to murder.
And Roderigo's progress from venial sins to mortal ones – from
lies and slander to killing – is another example of Iago's genius
for drawing people in. In this respect Roderigo serves as a foil
not for the ensign but for Othello himself. Both of them are
fooled by Iago, in both cases the object of the deception is
Desdemona, and in both cases they are gradually entangled in a
web of crime and deceit until it is too late to go back. Thus when
Roderigo finally decides, in Act IV, that he may as well give up
his quest it is too late: 'if she will return my jewels, I will give over
my suit,' he tells Iago, but this merely prompts his fellow con-
spirator to decide on his death, on the grounds that 'live
Roderigo,/He calls me to a restitution large . . .' (V, 1, 14–15),
and Iago has no intention of paying back the money and jewels
he has received for doing nothing.

Roderigo's mild rebellion against Iago in Act IV (see 2,
175–201) parallels Othello's doubts in Act III Scene 3, lines
365–79, when Othello demands proof of his wife's adultery.
Like Roderigo, Othello encompasses his own destruction by
trying to obtain something that cannot be had: in Roderigo's
case the love of a woman indifferent to him, in Othello's certainty about a sin that has not been committed. Roderigo's parallel with Othello is maintained throughout the play. When Iago
kills Roderigo, at the moment of death his dupe calls him an
'inhuman dog'; after Othello's death Lodovico addresses Iago as
a 'Spartan dog'. Similarly, the monetary images established by
Roderigo at the play's outset and constantly pursued by Iago in
their conversations, are echoed by Othello when he laments
Desdemona's supposed unfaithfulness, saying, for example, in
Act III Scene 3 'He that is robb'd, not wanting what is stolen/Let
him not know't and he's not robb'd at all'. (lines 348–9) Images
of money, of stealing and giving, are entwined throughout the
play with the idea of sexuality, sexual favours, betrayal and
constancy. Othello possesses Desdemona, but believes he does
not; Roderigo does not possess her and believes that he can.
Both of them see her as a commodity, and this is a moral and
spiritual failing in both.

Brabantio

> O, she deceives me
>
> Past thought!

Brabantio's love of his daughter is evident but it is a selfish possessive love, based on his parental authority built up over the years. His first thought on hearing that Desdemona has left him is for his own loss not for her safety. He must have kept her well guarded, for he is surprised that she has got out. Little did he understand her. And is Desdemona really so 'still and quiet' as he would have the Duke believe? Like many fathers, he resented the intrusion of any man who wished to take his daughter away from him; before her elopement with Othello, Brabantio had refused her to Roderigo and (presumably) others of the 'wealthy curled darlings' in whom, he deluded himself, she would have no interest, as she cared for her father so much. He resents Desdemona thinking more of any man than of him. Incidentally it was Brabantio who gladly invited Othello to his house, obviously under the impression that he would have no attraction for Desdemona. He therefore has only himself to blame for the outcome and this knowledge increases his anger. There is nothing so hard to bear in life as the results of our own misjudgement.

Brabantio is a powerful and influential man in Venice – he may, we are told, command at most houses. According to Iago (and therefore not necessarily true) he is

> much beloved,
>
> And hath in his effect a voice potential
>
> As double as the duke's.

But Brabantio labours under the misconception that everybody 'cannot but feel this wrong as 't were their own'. He does, however, accept the situation comparatively gracefully when Desdemona gives it as her choice.

The student may think that Brabantio is not important enough to be made the subject of a separate character study. Although Brabantio disappears after the first act, he is Desdemona's father, and had he not turned her out she might have stayed at home with his blessing until the war was over and might never have pleaded to go to Cyprus. His influence is probably felt throughout the play for, looking back, the audience naturally feels that when the war is over and Othello is no longer needed, it is Brabantio back in Venice who has now been successful in having him replaced. But he was not to live to see Othello's recall, Desdemona's 'match was mortal to him' in the meantime.

Brabantio's last words in the play are significant.

Look to her, Moor, if thou hast eyes to see:
She has deceived her father, and may thee.

Desdemona did not deceive the Moor, but it turned out to be true that the Moor had no eyes to see.

Structure

The structure of *Othello* is rendered less complicated than is usual in Shakespeare by the fact that there is no effective sub-plot. The only contender for this role – Roderigo's hopeless passion for Desdemona and Iago's attempts to turn this passion to his own advantage – is absorbed into the mainstream of the action by virtue of Iago's role in the play. In a sense the entire structure in terms of action is focused on the ensign, who initiates everything of significance, while the psychological weight of the play lies with Othello. The general's only two deeds of any note are (a) his victory over the Turks, which is peripheral to the main action and largely achieved by the agency of a chance storm; and (b) the murder of Desdemona, which is carried out by Othello, but instigated by Iago. Othello cannot be said to will either of these events. In other words, Iago acts while Othello reacts. It is partly this situation that helps to give the play its claustrophobic quality, as we watch Othello becoming increasingly helpless in a web of Iago's spinning.

But the claustrophobia also results from the concentration of the structure. This is to some extent the result of Shakespeare's plot treatment; it also owes a good deal to his presentation of relationships. The network of relationships is unusually close, all the main characters being directly involved with one another. Othello is married to Desdemona whose father Brabantio has been a friend. Cassio and Iago are his lieutenants, and Iago's wife Emilia is Desdemona's maid. Of the small cast of important parts only Roderigo and Bianca come from outside this tiny circle, but they are drawn into it because all the characters are also involved in complex relationships by virtue of their actual or supposed sexual liaisons: Othello with Desdemona and Emilia, Desdemona with Othello and Cassio, Cassio with Desdemona and Bianca, Roderigo with Desdemona, Iago with Emilia. And beyond these liaisons are the innumerable speculations about others, general or specific, in the speeches of Iago and Othello. The presentation of all the relationships is devoted to one structural end: the framing of the central links between Othello and Desdemona, and between Iago and

Othello. These in turn, both involving Othello as they do, point to him as the indisputable centre of attention in the play. Besides, all the relationships in the play are affected or even determined in one way or another by the character and circumstances of Othello. In Desdemona's case this is obvious, but we also learn from the play that, for example, Cassio conceals his relationship with Bianca from the general for fear of his displeasure; that Iago believes Othello to have slept with Desdemona and Emilia; and that Roderigo is jealous of Othello for taking Desdemona from him. All roads lead back to the hero. The same is true of the relationships between Cassio and Iago and Roderigo and Iago, both of which are conditioned by Iago's need for revenge against Othello, who is thus the passive focal point of all the action.

The clarity, energy and economy with which the sequence of events in the play are presented also make for structural concentration, and offer a striking contrast with the murky complexities explored in the psychological presentations of Othello and Iago. Nevertheless there is inevitably an interaction between physical and psychological events. The three major incidents of the play are Othello's marriage, which takes place before the action proper begins, Othello's victory over the Turks, which we do not see, and the murder of Desdemona, largely concealed from us by the marriage bed. The action which takes place on stage is all to do with Iago's plot: the rousing of Brabantio, Roderigo's fight with Cassio, the planting of the handkerchief, and so on. What really matters is the action in the minds of the characters, developed in the soliloquies and conversations of Iago and Othello, for the most part. Thus the simple structural outline is composed of Othello's physical actions – all in the heroic mould – and Iago's – all base – and this outline is filled out by psychological, emotional and spiritual developments. We can therefore refer more usefully to the structure of the play by thinking in terms of the stages through which Othello and Iago develop.

In Act I Othello carries all before him: he has married Desdemona, outfaced objections to the marriage, and found himself leading the Venetian fleet against the Turks by acclamation of the people. Iago is the underdog, beginning to hatch his plots. A hint of the changes to come is given by the framing of Othello's appearances in the first act by two lengthy conversations between Iago and Roderigo at the beginning and end. While the general has heroic presence, Iago has more to say, and his intimate manner and grim jocularity bring him closer to the audience at first than the grand remote Othello – whose very blackness sets him apart.

In Act II Othello reaches the high point of his career, victorious over the Turks and happily ecstatic in marriage. Iago is all the while brooding in the background: in the first two acts Othello's heroic stance is sharply contrasted with Iago's transition from unfocused resentment to the formulation of a strategy for revenge. In the first scene of Act I, this is merely a question of appearing to serve Roderigo by stirring up Brabantio against Othello. By the end of Act II Cassio's downfall has been engineered, and Iago has developed the main points of his plan to compromise Desdemona and thereby inflame Othello.

It is in Act III Scene 3 that the crucial reversal of their positions takes place: Iago establishes his mastery and Othello becomes the underdog. Structurally this is the central scene: appropriately it is the longest, most complex and subtle in the play. Here Shakespeare shows us what Cinthio does not: how Iago manages to persuade Othello that his lies are truth.

The rest of the play presents the working out of Iago's plot and Othello's continuing mental and spiritual deterioration, until the final climactic scene (Act V Scene 2) provides a structural balance with III, 3. Whereas the earlier scene shows the mystification of Othello and the darkening of his mind, V, 2 does the opposite: we witness the agonizing coming to terms of the hero with a truth he has never suspected. III, 3 and V, 2 have a corresponding intensity and weight: in each we explore the recesses of the hero's mind and witness the torture he experiences when torn between love and hate, trust and suspicion; each concentrates on the ambiguous nature of sexual passion.

When seen in terms of Othello's development and his waxing relationship with Iago the play falls into three stages: Othello's prosperity; Othello's mystification; Othello's enlightenment and catastrophe. These three stages are matched by the stages of: Iago's inferiority; Iago's dominance; Iago's discovery and downfall. They indicate the broad structural outline of the play.

Style

In the wider sense Shakespeare's style is determined by his preference for drama over lyric verse or prose narrative, blank verse over prose or rhyme, a richly coloured as opposed to a chaste diction, the proliferation of metaphor, enormous intellectual subtlety, and an intimate feeling for the ebb and flow of dramatic tension. All these points are relevant to the understanding of *Othello*.

Verse and prose

Shakespeare makes a number of distinctions between his uses of verse and prose. As a general rule prose is used for low-life and comic characters, verse for aristocrats, heroes and heroines; prose is associated with a lower plane of feeling, verse with a higher plane. In *Othello* the clown speaks in prose, whereas Brabantio has a relatively dignified verse style. But the distinction is by no means clear cut: Othello often speaks in prose, while Emilia's forthright and distinctly unaristocratic views on men and women (IV, 3, 84–103) are couched in sinuous formal verse. Rather than going only by character types the prose/verse division can be more reliably understood if we think of it as a question of what is appropriate: Othello speaks in prose when he is half crazed by hearing the conversation between Iago and Cassio in Act IV Scene 1, but he speaks in verse at the beginning of Act V Scene 2 when in an equally intense state. The difference between the two moments is decisive: in the first he is filled with furious disgust, in the second with a tragic sense of waste. The lyrical style is therefore appropriate to the loftiness of the second example, racy prose to the acrid fury of the first. Iago speaks his *soliloquies* in verse but much of his conversation in prose, especially with Roderigo. Much of the diction is similar but the verse form of the soliloquies heightens the intimacy of Iago's private thoughts, its formal style conflicting ironically with the hail-fellow-well-met manner of his public intercourse. The prose of his conversations with Roderigo is beautifully adapted to rapid changes of tone from bawdy to sinister, the racy colloquial diction again contrasting ironically with what the audience know of Iago's deliberation. Inwardness, unless it is the inwardness of madness, is almost always embodied by verse in Shakespeare; prose expresses the daily business of communication with others. Sometimes he will deliberately use verse to express thoroughly banal sentiments for comic effect, as when the Duke breaks into foolish rhyming couplets to give his good advice to Brabantio in Act I Scene 3 (202–9). The couplets are then sarcastically echoed by Brabantio. At other times the borders between verse and prose will be blurred. The last scene of the play is in verse throughout but the choked intensity of the emotions often threatens to break up the verse patterns into prose fragments: in Othello's speech (V, 2, 92–102) the verse only just holds together, and is thereby given the greater dramatic impact.

Idiom

Much of the richness of both verse and prose issues from the richness of the different idioms Shakespeare uses, from the flowery courtliness of Cassio at his most bombastic, to the salty phrases of Emilia. He exploits differences of style for dramatic purposes. Othello, for example, whose habitual manner of speech is incisive but dignified, sinks into colloquial, broken sentences and exclamations under the stress of finding his suspicions justified (IV, 1, 109–207). After the revelation of Iago's treachery in V, 2, he reverts to the nobility of his first speeches, as he recovers something of his old dignity and self-possession, especially in his final speech, when he says, 'I have done the state some service', recalling some of the first words he speaks in the play 'My services, which I have done the signiory.'

Desdemona has appropriate styles for speaking to the Duke (calm and dignified), to Othello (passionate and loving) and to Iago (friendly), which suggests not inconstancy on her part but a proper sense of propriety. She changes only her style, whereas Iago changes both his style and the substance of what he has to say: with Roderigo he is familiar and jocular; with Othello at first polite and confidential, then impertinent, sneering and domineering; with Desdemona he takes the role of the witty courtier; with Cassio that of the good friend. His style changes accordingly in each case. While Alexander Pope's claim cannot be sustained – that there is not a speech in Shakespeare inappropriate in style to the speaker at the moment of speaking – it is fair to say that at critical moments Shakespeare does find the right manner for the right character.

Flexibility and repetition

Within the limits of that general principle, and the limits imposed by the dominant rhythm of the iambic pentameter – the five-beat verse which had become the staple unit of English dramatic verse by Shakespeare's time – he achieves a remarkable degree of flexibility by breaking up lines, dividing them among characters, varying the rhythm, the use of an extensive vocabulary (over 24,000 words), repetition, and even the interruption of the verse flow. Take, for example, the lines (III, 4, 83–96) in which Othello is bullying Desdemona and she is falling into deeper and deeper trouble by espousing Cassio's cause.

Desdemona:	I say it is not lost.
Othello:	Fetch't, let me see it.
Desdemona:	Why, so I can sir, but I will not now,
	This is a trick, to put me from my suit,
	I pray let Cassio be receiv'd again.
Othello:	Fetch me that handkerchief, my mind misgives.
Desdemona:	Come, come,
	You'll never meet a more sufficient man.
Othello:	The handkerchief!
Desdemona:	I pray, talk me of Cassio.
Othello:	The handkerchief!
Desdemona:	A man that all his time
	Hath founded his good fortunes on your love,
	Shar'd dangers with you –
Othello:	The handkerchief!
Desdemona:	I'faith, you are to blame.
Othello:	Zounds!
Emilia:	Is not this man jealous?

Taken out of context, this can be seen as a commonplace domestic dispute: Othello pursues his unreasonable obsession with the handkerchief and Desdemona attempts to distract him with her own preoccupation. In context it embodies the collision between two kinds of ignorance: Desdemona dangerously inflames her husband's unsuspected temper and jealousy, while Othello lets his passions take over from his rational knowledge of the circumstances and his wife's character. It marks a disturbing

stage in Othello's progress to near insanity. Shakespeare regis-
ters these things not only in the placing of the incident within
the play, but also in the verse patterns. Notice the prepon-
derance of monosyllables, which allow great variety in the verse
stress patterns and greatly speed up the exchange, helping to
raise the emotional temperature. Notice also the divided lines,
the repetitions, the sharply cut-off line in which Othello is
reduced to swearing ('Zounds!') and the way in which he interrupts his wife. Within the formal framework of the verse this is a
highly naturalistic quarrel, the sound of two people not com-
municating. Shakespeare again uses the trick of repetition to
great effect in the final scene when the word 'husband' occurs
nine times, as Emilia unbelievingly echoes Othello's statement
that Iago told him Desdemona was false, and Othello irritably
echoes her repetition (see V, 2, 140–55).

Other techniques

Elsewhere we find the exploitation of very different techniques.
In Othello's earlier speeches, for example, the stifled collapse of
the later soliloquies is matched by a magnificent and stately
progress of the verse, as the hero exposes his heart and soul (see
I, 3, 128–70). In speeches such as this the structure is carefully
calculated: Othello tells his story with great skill, building up
from his polite reference to Brabantio: 'Her father lov'd me, oft
invited me', through a description of his adventures and Desdemona's response to them, to an effective answer to the charge of
witchcraft:

She lov'd me for the dangers I had pass'd,
And I lov'd her that she did pity them.
This only is the witchcraft I have us'd;

At which point Shakespeare makes Desdemona enter in a
theatrically telling climax to her husband's speech, 'Here comes
the lady, let her witness it.' This is a good example of Shakespeare's gift for putting the simplest theatrical strokes to good
use, postponing Desdemona's entry until we are curious to see
her.

Soliloquies

Iago's soliloquies offer another example of Shakespeare's theatrical skill. They exploit the convention that in the soliloquy the audience is overhearing the character's inmost thoughts to convey a quiet ferocity and take us into the complexities of a mind so used to deceit that it cannot distinguish between genuine hatred and detached enjoyment at the spectacle of suffering. Iago makes jokes that only we can understand, because only we, the audience, are in possession of all the facts. When in Act II Scene 3 he asks himself,

And what's he then, that says I play the villain,
When this advice I give is free, and honest,
Probal to thinking, and indeed the course
To win the Moor again?

he is amusing himself with such cynical reflections, but they are really for our benefit. Yet the joke is against him when he goes on to admit that Desdemona is 'fram'd as fruitful/As the free elements . . .', for with our knowledge of his character we know that he can never understand what this really means, so hateful and contemptible to him are all manifestations of virtue. Thus Iago's soliloquies have a double edge, revealing him in two senses: they show the workings of his plot but also demonstrate the weaknesses that are to prove his own downfall.

The soliloquy is one of the most important instruments by which Shakespeare reveals the inner life of his characters to the audience: it is a highly artificial theatrical convention, which allows the character to speak what he or she would normally only think. Before Shakespeare – in the work of Christopher Marlowe and Thomas Kyd – the soliloquy tended to be a stiff and formal affair, in which the character either addressed the audience directly, or showed an uncomfortable self-consciousness of their presence. Shakespeare's achievement was to give life to this convention by exploiting its possibilities for indirect self-revelation, irony, understatement, contradiction, free association, allusion, rich metaphor, the dramatic contrast of styles, rhythmic flexibility, the use of exclamations, questions, broken phrases, pauses, changes of tone and inflection. These developments must have gone together with a newer style of acting, advanced beyond the ranting and declaiming of the old school, so evident in Marlowe and Kyd, and of which Shakespeare makes fun, for instance in *Hamlet*, when Hamlet is coaching the actors in his play 'The Mousetrap'. Shakespeare's innovations also rested on the firm foundations laid by the great advances in English verse technique in the work of Spenser and Sidney, his immediate predecessors. Each soliloquy, while crucially placed within the play, has a life and form of its own, like a short dramatic poem. Even Iago's sardonic reflections have an intensity absent from the more general parts of the play.

It is in Othello's soliloquies, however, that we reach a height of dramatic power, rarely equalled, even by Shakespeare himself. Although Othello only has three soliloquies, two in the play's last scene, they are all important. In the great third scene of Act 3 we have the phenomenon of Iago acting almost as one of Othello's own inner voices: the dialogue between them often resembles a mind interrogating and tormenting itself. In the three soliloquies we are shown Othello's state of mind at three distinct stages. In the first (III, 3, 262–83) the hero is on the brink of believing in his wife's guilt: he is still in the state of pride which thinks only of his own pain and shame at the possibility of her adultery, not of Desdemona's condition or the possible reasons for it. In the second stage (V, 2, 1–22) he has reached the point of trying to reconcile the opposites of love and hatred in his mind (for an extended analysis of this speech see the following section on 'Language and imagery'). In the third (V, 2, 92–102) he is almost incoherent with remorse. Each is different in style: the first is reflective, the second intensely lyrical, and the third exclamatory – these three styles reflecting the progressive deterioration in Othello's state. They each mark a moment at which the action pauses for the hero to consider his condition before some inexorable next step – the conviction of guilt, the murder, and discovery of the murder.

Acting

Soliloquy is not Shakespeare's only form of set piece. His plays almost invariably involve some form of music or mime. Besides the entertainment value of these episodes in themselves, they reveal Shakespeare as a highly self-aware artist fascinated by theatrical conventions, and the ways in which they can be made to embody feelings and ideas, or to convey the dramatic sense. In *Othello* this fascination shows up in two ways. One is through the self-conscious acting skills of Iago, who delights not only in fooling the other characters for his own purposes, but in the process of fooling itself, teasing both Roderigo and Othello, when he has them in his power. Iago is, after all, a kind of actor: 'I am not what I am' he says, pointing up Shakespeare's pre-occupation with the theme of identity and the ways in which the actor's task is symbolic of the perplexing difference between appearance and reality. Even at the end of the play, when he refuses to speak, Iago is playing a part, exercising his power over the other characters in one last desperate refusal to tell them the truth – something he has concealed throughout.

Music

Shakespeare's interest in theatrical devices also shows up in the scenes with music. They are very different, but both significant. In Act II, Scene 3 Iago's object is to get Cassio drunk and involve him in a discreditable fight with three Cypriots and Roderigo. To urge on the party spirit, he sings two drinking songs. These reveal Iago in a somewhat unlikely role as 'one of the boys' – but the strangeness of this simply reminds us what a good 'actor' Iago is. They also introduce a certain light relief, and the bois-terous, crude fun conflicts sharply with Othello's dignity, which cuts into the scene when he enters to quell the brawl, contrasting his heroic stature with the foolish Cassio, and giving Iago a chance to play yet another role, that of the sincere friend.

Incomparably more powerful, however, is Act IV Scene 3, in which Desdemona sings. If Iago reveals a bluff masculinity in his drinking songs, nothing could more effectively show up Desde-mona's girlish vulnerability than her unaccompanied melan-choly song in the dead of night, as she prepares, unknowingly, for her last sleep. When Emilia later quotes the song, citing the example of the swan that is supposed to sing only before its death (just before *her* own death), the moment reverberates restrospectively in our minds back to the song we heard a few minutes earlier. Quite apart from the appropriateness of the words, it is the fact that Desdemona sings at all which is so important, providing a moment of lyrical calm before the final storm, much as Othello's second soliloquy does at the beginning of Act V Scene 2. (Ophelia too sang while floating to her death.)

Shakespeare was not alone in using music, and the aspects of theatrical spectacle associated with it. Other Jacobean dramatists do the same. But he uses it with a fine sense of the dramatically appropriate and as an essential part of a style that manages to resolve the most varied constituents into a unity of effect, all the more powerful because *Othello* is a play in which *visual* spectacle plays relatively little part.

Language and imagery

We have discussed the structure and style of the play, but these mean little in Shakespeare's case unless they are related to the unique quality of his linguistic practice. As is well-known, each Shakespeare play, whether from design or not we cannot know, exhibits a characteristic patterning of images, recurring words and phrases, which reinforce the overall design and subtly comment on it. While it is impossible to assess finally the impact of such verbal elements, which depend a good deal on the perceptiveness of the individual reader or viewer, it is possible to point out dominant threads of imagery and some of the ways in which they relate to the play as a whole. When doing this it is also helpful to remember that on the linguistic level we are responding to the play in at least two distinguishable ways: as a complete dramatic action and as a dramatic poem; in the first case the words are a medium, in the second they are everything. To some extent, our response to the work as a play or as a poem depends on whether we see it or read it; but much of the interest and the difficulty of Shakespeare's work issue from the fact that the two cannot be finally separated. As in a piece of music, the sounds point to a structure beyond themselves and yet are themselves the music.

Metaphor

While *Othello* does not have the luxuriant imagery to be found in *Hamlet* or *Antony and Cleopatra*, it is nevertheless an exceptionally subtle and complex linguistic pattern. As in all Shakespeare's work, the dominant feature of the language in *Othello* is its metaphoric quality. *Metaphor* is not merely the comparison of two different things with each other, but their close identification. When Iago says, for example, 'Thus do I ever make my fool my purse' (I, 3, 381), he is not merely saying that he profits financially from other people's foolishness; he is making an equation between human qualities and material ones that says something about both. In this case Iago is telling us that, on the one hand, taking advantage of things is just a matter of using intelligence, and on the other, that the only use of intelligence is to make sure you look after yourself. The phrase is especially suggestive here because it comes after Iago has repeatedly advised Roderigo to 'put money' in his purse, i.e. used the very same words to tell Roderigo to look to *his* own advantage. Roderigo is not bright enough to work out that if Iago is deceiving others he may very well be deceiving him, but Iago can enjoy the joke. Here the metaphor unites the irony of Iago's betrayal of Roderigo with the immorality of Iago's precept — always look after yourself at the expense of others — in a way that reflects on both Roderigo's foolishness and Iago's apparent cleverness. Metaphor has this highly suggestive and even ambiguous quality, which is especially important to *Othello*, a play in which familiar words and ideas are constantly presented in unlikely new guises.

Appearance and reality

Take, for example, the word 'honest'. The surface level of the irony with which this word is used is obvious: Othello constantly refers to Iago as an honest man when we know that he is the very opposite. But the word's role in the play is far more complex than at first appears. Iago frequently uses the word to describe himself. When he says to Cassio, 'As I am an honest man . . .' (II, 3, 258), he is sharing a joke with the audience; and the joke is on Cassio, who agrees with him. Iago enjoys such games. On the other hand, when he sneers at 'honest knaves' (I, 1, 49) he is using the word in its proper sense to condemn those who foolishly put virtue and truth before self-interest — using it, in other words, as a term of contempt. The word takes on a complex significance through constant repetition. When Cassio bids good night to 'honest Iago' (II, 3, 341) Iago reverses the meaning of the word a few lines later when he again sardonically refers to himself as honest, knowing full well what he is. This irony spreads through the play. Desdemona refers to Cassio's 'honest face' (III, 3, 50), though we know he is deceiving her and Othello about Bianca, and even contributes unknowingly to her destruction. Desdemona hopes that 'my noble lord esteems me honest' (IV, 2, 65) even as Othello is preparing her doom; and when Emilia insists that her mistress is indeed honest (IV, 2, 12) Othello refuses to believe it. The two poles of vice and virtue in the play are Iago and Desdemona: Iago is consistently praised for his honesty; Desdemona is consistently suspected for her dishonesty.

Othello's confusion about the word reaches a climax in Act III Scene 3 when he concludes: 'I think my wife be honest, and think she is not' (line 390), and at this point we need to note that besides its ironic complexity 'honest' also has complexity by definition: it can mean not only truthful, but also sexually chaste. Besides these meanings it also has a patronizing sense referring to social inferiors as a term of praise. Iago uses it in all three senses and plays on them. Othello's line quoted above clearly uses two senses: honest and chaste. We must also remember that the word does not exist on its own: it is part of the linguistic and conceptual network without which it would have no meaning. We only have a sense for honest because we have the concept of dishonesty. So the various usages of the word encourage us to think about the different notions of honesty explored in the play and their relevance for the different characters. Emilia's notion of honesty, for example, is very different from Desdemona's; Emilia has lower standards and a more relaxed attitude to morality.

The word 'honest' is also linked to a whole group of words and images that have to do with appearance and reality: seeming, looking, concealing, disguise, frankness, misunderstanding and deception are all ideas which recur. The distinction between being and seeming is a major theme. Othello several times proclaims himself as one who is what he appears: 'My parts, my title, and my perfect soul/Shall manifest me rightly' (I, 2, 31–2). Iago, on the other hand, exults in concealing his true nature: 'I am not what I am' (I, 1, 65).

Again, these are two poles of truth and deception between which the play moves, though neither is what it seems: Othello is wrong to think that everything in our natures can be simply manifested, just as Iago is wrong to believe that we can completely conceal our true intentions. Both of them reveal aspects of their nature not understood by them: Othello is seduced by his jealous frenzy; Iago carried away by the exhilaration of his plotting. However, we can measure Othello's decline in terms of his own ideal of frankness. By Act III Scene 3 he is asking Iago to: set on/Thy wife to observe' (lines 243–4) and in Act IV Scene 1 he hides to watch Iago's conversation with Cassio.

At the end of the play all ways of seeming are shown up for what they are by the light of truth – the revelation of Iago's deception, which drives the villain himself into silence; his tongue, which has been the main instrument of deception, is no longer of any use. Yet until this moment, the theme of appearance and reality is developed even at the height of the hero's crisis, in the language he uses. When Othello realizes what he has done, 'Now: how dost thou look now?' (V, 2, 273) he asks of Desdemona's corpse, having earlier killed her on the basis of visual evidence: 'I saw my handkerchief in his hand . . .' (V, 2, 63). Deceived by appearances, Othello is finally stricken with the sight of his dead wife. But this appearance is irreversible reality: she *is* dead, even though she *seems* to live for a moment when Emilia comes in. Like many in the play, this scene takes place at night.

The text is filled with images of darkness, confusion, uncertainty and perplexity. It is also full of violent oppositions: love and hate; heaven and hell; light and dark; life and death; black and white; blood and stars; cruelty and kindness; guilt and innocence. It is on this level that the play and the dramatic poem are one, the conflicts of the play reflecting the larger oppositions of life itself. This is made clear in Othello's great soliloquy at the beginning of Act V Scene 2. He is naturally in a state of painful excitement – a man used to killing, but only in war, still passionately in love with his wife and acutely conscious of her physically, yet consumed with jealous doubts. The only way to make sure of certainty is for Othello to kill her: then she can betray no more men, i.e. Othello himself. Yet to kill her is to lose the very thing he values most; to satisfy his doubts he must part with their object. This is the play's most erotically charged moment. It is dark and he speaks quietly: the involved syntax reflects the tormented twisting and turning of his mind as he moves between pity and determination, love and hate, desire and jealousy, all too aware of the finality of the deed he proposes to commit. The speech is full of those violent oppositions noted above, which contribute to its resonance: this is not just Othello on the terrible brink of killing his wife, but any human being on the brink of an inevitable and disastrous act which he knows to be irreversible, destructive of his own happiness yet irresistible, driven to it by unbearable conflict. At the end of the soliloquy, as Desdemona wakes to her last sleep, Othello says

So sweet was ne'er so fatal: I must weep,
But they are cruel tears; this sorrow's heavenly,
It strikes when it does love: she wakes . . .

and his last words recall the proud reference to Desdemona's arrival in the council chamber (I, 3, 170) with which Othello ended the speech announcing to the senators the happiness of his marriage.

Oxymoron

Fatal sweetness, cruel tears, heavenly sorrow, murderous love: these are all examples of oxymoron, a figure of speech popular in 16th-century poetry, combining contradictory terms. Shakespeare here makes explicit a process we can trace throughout the play, in which this figure of speech plays a vital part: the attempt to synthesize or reconcile opposites, especially noticeable in Iago. At the very beginning of the play, for example, Iago speaks of Cassio being 'damn'd in a fair wife' (I, 1, 21), and a few lines later refers to 'honest knaves' (I, 1, 49) who do 'themselves homage' (I, 1, 54), declaring that 'I am not what I am.' (I, 1, 65). He speaks of 'poisoning delight' (I, 1, 69) and 'the beast with two backs' (I, 1, 116). His whole manner of speech is soaked in such expressions, until at the very end of the play he tacitly confesses his guilt by the contradictory means of remaining silent – a paradox for the talkative Iago if ever there was one. Elsewhere he speaks of the 'Divinity of hell' (II, 3, 341) and the double-faced god Janus (I, 2, 33) who are his tutelary deities. It is in their spirit of contradiction that he infects Othello and turns the general's reality on its head. Thus, in the middle of the play (III, 3) Othello begins to employ the animal and vermin imagery, previously reserved for Iago.

Verbal echoes and repetitions in imagery

Oxymoron is appropriate to a play full of contradictions, yet it is only the most subtle of the many linguistic patterns in *Othello*. Easier to trace, perhaps, are the verbal echoes and repetitions enforcing the play's many interlocked themes. Images of poisoning; of the marriage bed (mentioned in every act); of wealth and of buying and selling; of the devil; of eyes and looks; of the army; of sexuality and fickleness of women; of animals –

all these abound. Sometimes they are especially associated with one character: the devil with Iago, purity and its opposite with Desdemona, the monster of jealousy with Othello. In this sense the imagery enforces the dramatic outline. But in another sense these chains of images create the verbal texture that is the dramatic poem, irrespective of who uses them.

Language is a communal activity and all the characters participate in its expression, even minor ones such as Lodovico who have no dramatic significance in their own right, but who contribute to the play's poetic wholeness. So it is that Lodovico, for example, has the play's last lines, which allude to a cluster of words and images which thread through the work.

> O Spartan dog,
> More fell than anguish, hunger, or the sea,
> Look on the tragic lodging of this bed:
> This is thy work, the object poisons sight,
> Let it be hid: Gratiano, keep the house,
> And seize upon the fortunes of the Moor,
> For they succeed to you: to you, lord governor,
> Remains the censure of this hellish villain,
> The time, the place, the torture: O, enforce it!
> Myself will straight aboard, and to the state
> This heavy act with heavy heart relate. (V, 2, 363–72)

Here, in a few lines, we have the animal image persistently used by Iago and now applied to him; we have the marriage bed, which now holds the corpses of husband and wife, united in death as in love; we have the notion of sight – the appearance – being poisoned, and the idea of concealment; we have Iago addressed as a devil, a hellish villain; and so on. The references might be multiplied, but the point is clear: the complex verbal texture not only holds the play together and supports the main lines of the action, it also has a life of its own. Even such a passing mention as that to the sea can awaken in the reader or hearer memories of the sea's role earlier in the play: as the scene of Othello's great victory over the Turks, or the source of the ominous storm which portends a storm in the lives of the characters. Or we may recall the association of the sea with Desdemona in Cassio's words suggesting the benevolence of fortune to her: 'Tempests themselves, high seas and howling winds . . ./do omit/ Their common natures, letting go safely by/The divine Desdemona' (II, 1, 68–73).

In II, 1, 187–93 the sea suggests, in a way that is to prove ironic, the calm before the storm: 'And let the labouring bark . . ./ . . . not another comfort, like to this/Succeeds in unknown fate.' In III, 3, 460–7, 'Like to the Pontic Sea . . ./Swallow them up', Othello is set on revenge. Later in the play, Othello uses another image of the sea to imply that Desdemona is out of touch with natural things, a wanton, as free with her sexual favours as 'The bawdy wind that kisses all it meets . . .' (IV, 2, 80).

In this respect, Lodovico's reference to Iago's cruelty as worse than the sea's — just before he himself sets sail for Venice — reminds us of the imagery's protean nature in *Othello*, which depends upon the ambivalent nature of language as a medium on the one hand common to all speakers, and on the other used by individuals for their own purposes. It is this ambivalence that helps to generate much of the play's irony, resulting as it so often does, from the use of normal words in abnormal contexts; and it is to *irony* that we must turn our attention next.

Irony

Irony arises when the literal sense of words is contradicted by their deeper meaning. *Dramatic irony* results when either the speaker of the words or the person to whom they are addressed is ignorant of their true meaning (which is apparent to the audience, then or later). Othello's constant references to Iago's honesty, for example, are ironic in one way, because the audience know the truth about Iago; Iago's own references to his honesty are ironic in another way because he knows the truth too. Othello's irony is unintentional, Iago's deliberate. When Othello uses the word, the irony is tragic, because of what is to come; when Iago uses it, there is a strong vein of satirical black humour apparent. But it so happens that both the characters are in the dark about their own fate, so the irony is double. Even the audience do not know 'the full facts' until the play is over, and then the deeper questions remain. Why did these people act in this way? What is the meaning of their lives and fates, if any?

Irony depends upon someone's ignorance – ignorance of the true meaning of what is said or what is to come. It is natural that a play that takes ignorance for one of its 'themes' should be ironic through and through. Not one of the characters really knows any of the others. And because irony depends upon context, because it requires that the audience know more than the characters, it deepens as the play develops. When, for example, Iago says near the beginning of the play that 'I am not what I am', we take this at first to be simply a play on words, expressing his intention to deceive Othello. It is only later that a deeper significance dawns on us, and we realize that it refers not only to Iago's deception of others but to his self-deception, and to the deep-seated insecurity and doubts about his identity which help to generate the hatred and bitterness that drive him on. He takes a delight in negation, in destruction: he is not what he is, because he is the spirit of 'No', opposed to the 'yes'-saying spirit of Desdemona's love for Othello. Iago frequently reiterates the notion that he is other than he seems: as the play progresses we compare these comments with Othello's claims to the opposite, to being completely revealed in his appearance:

'My parts, my title and my perfect soul/Shall manifest me rightly
...' (I, 2, 31–2), he says, and we believe him – until his faith
begins to appear misplaced when Iago's hints about Desdemona
reveal another Othello. His earlier claims then sound ironic in
retrospect – which makes the point that dramatic irony works
both forward and backward. Only when we reach the end of the
play is Othello's self-possession partly restored, but by then the
theme of Othello's achievement of self-knowledge is bound up
with the theme of Iago's deceptions by a complex web of ironic
references

Relational and situational irony

Irony is not only verbal, especially in a play: it depends also on
the relationships of the characters and the disposition of the
parts of the action. We might call these two kinds of irony
relational and *situational*. To take the play's most obvious example
of relational irony: Othello's relationship to Iago is evidently
ironic. This remains the case even when the ensign's treachery is
revealed, because Iago is in one sense successful: he brings about
the downfall of Desdemona and Othello, though it be at the cost
of his own life. There is also a situational irony here, because it is
precisely the disclosure that Othello has been fooled which gives
him the final push towards suicide. In other words, Othello and
Iago are in a definitively ironic relationship, and this puts them
into ironic situations. Iago's situation at the end is just as ironic
as Othello's: they both retreat into silence by different routes,
but Iago's allows him to maintain the confusion he has created
by his words because he refuses to clear it up with more words.
The relationships of Cassio and Desdemona with Iago are also
ironic because of their ignorance of his true nature: this means
they are constantly at cross-purposes in conversation. The same
is true of Roderigo. But the most powerful relational and situational ironies arise from the tragic misunderstanding between
Othello and Desdemona. In Act III Scene 4, for example, we
find both are ignorant of the true circumstances, pursuing
unfortunate obsessions (lines 28–95): the very triviality of the
handkerchief on which Othello harps emphasizes the pathos.
The handkerchief recurs at a crucial moment in Act II Scene 5,
just before the murder: 'That handkerchief which I so lov'd and
gave thee ...' he says, unconsciously making the point that he

has come to value his own certainty (i.e. the handkerchief) more than his wife's life. The irony operates on several levels here: the audience know that it is Othello who is betraying a trust, not his wife, and that he is preferring the evidence of just those unreliable senses he condemns in her (he says he 'saw' the handkerchief in Cassio's hand) to the evidence his heart and reason give him.

By expressing the ridiculous idea that one can 'love' a handkerchief Othello betrays the monumental distortion of his values by jealousy. What he loves is his own self-esteem: this is what he mistakenly hopes to preserve by killing his wife, so that she cannot betray him 'again'. This use of the handkerchief is a fine example of Shakespeare's method, not only because it shows how the irony is cumulative throughout the play – when we first hear of the handkerchief it is as no more than a piece of planted evidence – but because it demonstrates in performance how he is able to give a trivial object more significance and dramatic weight than analysis can reveal. In other words, the emotional import of the handkerchief transcends anything one can say about it: the ironic passes into the untranslatable tragic experience which only the audience can have by witnessing the play as a performance through time.

Irony in plot and structure

Besides verbal, relational and situational ironies, there are also ironic dimensions to the plot and structure of the play. We have already considered some of these (see under 'Plot' and 'Structure'), but there are many others. When Desdemona elects to accompany Othello to Cyprus she cannot know that she is going voluntarily to the place of her own doom. When Roderigo agrees to kill Cassio for Iago he signs his own death-warrant. When Othello listens to slanders against his wife it is his own character that is implicitly being shown up as untrustworthy, and he ultimately brings about his own downfall. When Iago plans the destruction of others he ensures his own. When Emilia keeps quiet about Iago's odd desire for the handkerchief she is preparing the way for her outburst at the end of the play: her refusal to enquire into Iago's fantasy leads to a horrific fulfilment of that fantasy, including her own death. When Cassio begs Desdemona to intercede with Othello for his future, he is securing not life but death. All these are examples of ironically contradicted intentions in the plot.

The structure too is ironic, especially in its use of parallels. Iago sets out to betray the General's wife and is finally brought down by his own. Othello's lack of trust in Desdemona enacts in himself the very betrayal of trust he suspects in her. Bianca's suspicion of Cassio and her entry with the handkerchief while Othello is watching, help to bring her not Cassio's love but his near death, while Emilia, who advises Desdemona that women should behave as cynically as men do, is doomed – by the unexpected strength of her disinterested love for her mistress, as Desdemona is by the strength of *her* love for Othello, and Othello by the strength of *his* passion for his wife. Most ironically of all, the detached Iago is betrayed by the strength of his passions; envy, hatred and bitterness.

Irony related to ideas and themes

Finally, the play communicates a penetrating level of irony on the conceptual and thematic level, i.e. in the way contradictory ideas are developed. Take the opposite notions of *speech and silence*. At the opening of the play we notice that Iago is highly skilled with words: he spins brilliant chains of images and reasoning, seems able to express his inmost thoughts, and persuade others to his will – though he describes himself as a plain man of action. Yet at the end of the play he refuses to speak: 'Demand me nothing, what you know, you know/From this time forth I never will speak word' (V, 2, 304–5). Othello too presents himself as a plain soldier yet he too can express himself with great eloquence, until the moment when he is persuaded of Desdemona's infidelity. Words desert him and he faints; words, which helped to betray him, well might he mistrust them. Emilia, however, who is described by Desdemona as having 'no speech' (II, 2, 103) proves to be a formidably effective verbal performer when she tears the veil from Iago in the play's last scene. Yet at the moment of death it is a song she recalls: the song in which Desdemona gave poignant expression to her fears – fears that she loves Othello too much to say so directly.

As it happens, Othello acknowledges the power of Desdemona's singing earlier in the play, describing her as an 'admirable musician' and one who will 'sing the savageness out of a bear' (IV, 1, 184), yet she fails to talk the savageness out of the bear Othello in the last scene. Indeed, it is while Desdemona is begging him to stay his hand 'but while I say one prayer' that he kills her. One of the cruellest ironies associated with Desdemona is that even in death Othello refers not to her words – in which she always spoke the truth – but to her appearance, which he takes to be the source and therefore the *evidence* of her attractiveness for, and attraction to other men – recalling Iago's line about Cassio being 'damn'd in a fair wife'. Othello himself remarks that it 'is not words that shake me thus. Pish! Noses, ears and lips!' (IV, 1, 41). This comment is sadly vindicated by his refusal to listen to Desdemona's words. Yet it is by Iago's words that he has been betrayed. The irony here is complex and encompassing. Only in the very last line of the play, when Lodovico says that he will 'to the state/With heavy heart this heavy act relate . . .' (V, 2, 371–2), can we once again trust in the truthfulness of words. But by then all that remains for Othello is silence: the words are other people's.

General questions

1 Write on Shakespeare's management of the plot of *Othello*.

Suggested notes for essay answer:
Simplicity – stark economy and outline (contrast with psychological complexity) – two *motifs* (love and revenge) – love to jealousy to revenge (cf. Othello and Roderigo.)
Plot = revenge drama on one level. Iago – Cassio and Othello – Iago as initiator. Five acts = five stages of plot. I – Roderigo and conspiracy. II Cassio's disgrace. III Othello's jealousy. IV This jealousy strengthened by Cassio/Bianca talking; the handkerchief. V Desdemona's death – Iago's guilt.

Refer back briefly to Cinthio's *The Moor of Venice*, indicate Shakespeare's treatment of it: differences; expansions etc; concentrations etc. Dramatic economy and intensity, theatrical effects – the poisoning of Othello's mind (III, 3), Desdemona's last conversation with Emilia (IV, 3). Effect of last scene – whole series of dramatic incidents piled one on the other – murder, exposure, suicide – powerful ending. Varies speed of plot exposition – contrast slow sequences (III, 3) with fast (V, 2). Superb control of climax.

2 Outline and discuss the time scheme of *Othello*, showing why the *impression* of the time taken by the play differs from it.

3 So will I turn her virtue into pitch,
And out of her own goodness make the net
That shall enmesh them all.
How does Iago achieve his aim?

4 *Othello* has been attacked as pessimistic. How far do you consider the charge true?

5 What do you find to admire in the character of Othello?

6 How far is it true to say that Othello owes his ruin to his suspicion?

7 'Where is this rash and most unfortunate man?' asks Lodovico. How far do you consider Othello rash and how far unfortunate?

8 'Othello has a poet's imagination and speaks with a poet's tongue.' Comment on this statement, paying particular attention to the imagery of Othello's language.

9 How far is Desdemona responsible for the catastrophe of *Othello*?

10 It is the peculiar excellence of Shakespeare's heroines that they seem to exist only in their attachment to others. They are pure abstractions of the affections. We think as little of their persons as they do themselves, because we are let into the secrets of their hearts, which are more important. (Hazlitt)

To what extent is this true of Desdemona?

11 Write on Iago's genius for villainy.

12 What reasons does Iago give for his hatred of Othello, and how far do these reasons seem to you to be the real ones?

13 What part is played by Cassio in developing the plot of *Othello*?

14 'Of all Shakespeare's tragedies . . . not even excepting *King Lear, Othello* is the most painfully exciting and the most terrible.' Account for this.

15 How far is *Othello* a tragedy of bad luck and how far a tragedy of just retribution?

16 Is it true to say that in *Othello* character is destiny?

17 Do you think that *Othello* is sensational rather than tragic? Discuss the question fully.

18 'A good play has in it a variety of life and character.' Does *Othello* meet this condition?

19 For what purposes does Shakespeare use prose in *Othello*?

20 Coleridge says that Shakespeare uses expectation rather than surprise for dramatic effect. Illustrate this from *Othello*.

21 'The truth is that Shakespeare's best things are not very effective on the stage.' Give your opinion on this statement with reference to *Othello*.

22 '*Othello* is great as literature and great as drama.' Illustrate how the two aspects are fused in the play.

23 In what ways was *Othello* influenced by the stage for which Shakespeare wrote?

Further reading

W. H. Auden: *The Dyer's Hand* (Faber, 1962), the essay called 'The Joker in the Pack', a provocative and brilliant commentary on the play. Only for the advanced student.

John Bayley: *The Characters of Love* (Constable, 1960), has a long and subtle essay on *Othello* which considers the three main characters in relation to the theme of love.

A. C. Bradley: *Shakespearean Tragedy* (Macmillan, 1904). Particularly good on character.

H. Granville Barker: *Prefaces to Shakespeare*: *Othello* (Sidgwick & Jackson, 1949). A long, detailed, intelligent discussion of the play, bearing in mind the actor's and director's point of view.

R. B. Heilman *Magic in the Web*: *Action and language in Othello* (Greenwood Press, 1977). A detailed study of imagery.

J. Wain ed. *Shakespeare's Othello* (Macmillan, 1971). Includes an excellent survey of criticism by the editor.